Bigger Isn't Always Better

A Leadership Guide for Small School Administrators

George Murdock

ROWMAN & LITTLEFIELD EDUCATION
A division of
ROWMAN & LITTLEFIELD PUBLISHERS, INC.
Lanham • New York • Toronto • Plymouth, UK

Published by Rowman & Littlefield Education
A division of Rowman & Littlefield Publishers, Inc.
A wholly owned subsidiary of The Rowman & Littlefield Publishing Group, Inc.
4501 Forbes Boulevard, Suite 200, Lanham, Maryland 20706
http://www.rowmaneducation.com

Estover Road, Plymouth PL6 7PY, United Kingdom

Copyright © 2012 by George Murdock

All rights reserved. No part of this book may be reproduced in any form or by any electronic or mechanical means, including information storage and retrieval systems, without written permission from the publisher, except by a reviewer who may quote passages in a review.

British Library Cataloguing in Publication Information Available

Library of Congress Cataloging-in-Publication Data

Murdock, George, 1942-
Bigger isn't always better : a leadership guide for small school administrators / George Murdock.
p. cm.
Includes bibliographical references and index.
ISBN 978-1-61048-720-7 (cloth : alk. paper) -- ISBN 978-1-61048-721-4 (pbk. : alk. paper) -- ISBN 978-1-61048-722-1 (electronic)
1. School administrators--United States. 2. Small schools--United States. 3. School management and organization--United States. 4. Educational leadership--United States. I. Title.
LB2831.82.M87 2012
371.2--dc23

2011046713

♾ The paper used in this publication meets the minimum requirements of American National Standard for Information Sciences Permanence of Paper for Printed Library Materials, ANSI/NISO Z39.48-1992.

Printed in the United States of America

"It is estimated that among administrators who lose their jobs, about ninety-eight percent fail in the arena of human relations issues and two percent fail because of a lack of technical expertise."

With all due respect to the complex equation education has become, the most important element in successful small school leadership is common sense.

This book is written for the tens of thousands of administrators who work in small school districts across the country—the districts of 1,500 students or less which make up approximately 75 percent of America's school units.

Contents

Preface		vii
Introduction		ix
1	Perpetuating Small Schools	1
2	Getting (And Keeping) The Job: The Transition From Training To Employment	11
3	Creating An Entry Plan	25
4	Effective Leadership and Decision-Making Practices	35
5	Board-Superintendent Relations	45
6	Developing An Effective Format For Board Meetings, *Or* "Nothing Good Happens After 8 p.m."	57
7	Creating An Administrative Evaluation System	61
8	Creating An Effective Communication Program	67
9	Building A Foundation For Effective Relations and Understanding Rural Communities	73
10	Building a Foundation For Effective Staff Relations	85
11	Maintenance and Facilities	93
12	Fiscal Management	99
13	Human Resources and Negotiations	105
14	Instructional Leadership and Student Achievement	115
About the Author		121

Preface

In the late 1930s, fresh out of the University of Washington, my father was hired to teach social studies and coach football at Winlock High School, about 100 miles south of Seattle.
It was the beginning of a long career that would lead him into school administration and into a series of small school districts. His family followed him from Winlock to Castle Rock, where he became a principal and then to Toledo where he was the superintendent. I started school in Castle Rock and moved to Toledo at the end of the seventh grade. I graduated from Toledo High School in a class of thirty-seven.
When we moved to Castle Rock in the 1950s, there were three grocery stores, several men's and ladies apparel shops, two hardware stores, numerous restaurants, a soda fountain and candy store, a car dealer, a lumber yard, an appliance store, and various other businesses. Most of them are now gone.
Castle Rock is like many small towns across America where the heart of the business district has vanished and in some cases, only the school remains.
In December of 2009, I returned to Toledo to bury my mother. There's still a grocery store, a service station, a restaurant, a tavern, and several second-hand stores. Many of the other businesses are history. Perhaps Toledo is lucky to have some semblance of a business community.
We held a luncheon at the church for the family and friends who came to honor my mom. The walls of Toledo Presbyterian Church are lined with a stunning array of stained glass windows—each in memory of pillars of the church who are now gone. They provide a weekly reminder that the foundation of the church and the community it serves is rooted more in history than in the future.

Although the place where I grew up is something of a shadow of its former self, I'm grateful for the experience of having grown up in small towns like Toledo, Winlock, and Castle Rock. They represent thousands of small communities across America—each with their own unique history, landmarks, traditions, and customs.

They are indeed the heart of America and those who remain realize the school is virtually the last vestige of their identity and they would do practically anything to preserve it.

While all school administrators are well-advised to invest time in both learning and monitoring the underlying values and norms which are prevalent in the communities they serve, it is particularly important to do so in small, rural settings where such issues play a critical role in the operation of the school.

My father was a typical rural school administrator.

If the bleachers needed to be swept before a game, he picked up a broom. Whenever he walked around a school building or across a campus, he invariably would go out of his way to pick up a loose pop can or a lunch sack. Every night at about 10 p.m., he and my mother would drive through the city park to make sure everything was in order because the schools and the community were completely intertwined.

He helped coach the football team, opened up the school on a Sunday afternoon if someone needed in and organized work parties to help enhance the facilities. He was willing to help young teachers get a start because he knew that while some of them would eventually move on to larger systems, his best chance of finding the cream of the crop was at their graduation.

He served as chairman of Cheese Days for more than thirty years, he was president of the Lions Club, he spearheaded the creation of the city park, he talked the county commissioners into building tennis courts next to the high school, he helped with canned food drives, he delivered baskets to the needy at Thanksgiving and Christmas, and he helped build several athletic fields. The gymnasium at Toledo High School is named in his honor.

While he had the opportunity to move on to larger systems and more pay, his heart was in small schools where he knew the students and their parents and where he could be involved in every aspect of the equation.

Like so many of the people who live in small, rural communities, the value of place superseded the possibilities of more income.

I treasure the opportunity to have spent my formative years attending small schools and living in small communities and I remain proud to say I graduated from a very small high school.

Perhaps the opportunity to write a book about working in small schools is a way of helping to pay back those who were willing to work there and contribute to my education.

Introduction

Working in a small school is not for the timid or the lazy. While there is a desperate need to expand the pool of strong candidates for small school leadership positions, it is also important to create a sense of reality and understanding among those who would prepare themselves for such an assignment. With declining resources and expanding expectations, rural school leaders are finding themselves pulled in a variety of directions.

The purpose of this book is to provide small school administrators with thoughts, ideas, and experiences gathered from dozens of small schools and the leaders who have served them. The topics range from strategies for landing the job and the development of an entry plan to practices in terms of effective leadership and working with the school board.

Later chapters address the important subject of communication and understanding the community as well as the development of effective staff relations. The final chapters are devoted to specific areas of responsibility such as maintenance and facilities, fiscal management, human resource management, and instructional leadership.

WEARING A VARIETY OF HATS

An article in the October 2003 edition of *School Administration* focused on the "double duty" aspects of the principalship and superintendency in small districts. Noted the article, "resource-squeezed school chiefs in remote towns often find themselves driving buses, filling in as substitute teachers, overseeing school activities, and even helping in the lunchroom."

Many school administrators working in smaller communities become well aware of the fact that their job isn't just a way of life, it becomes their life. But for those who understand both the positive and negative aspects of this phenomenon, it can become a very wonderful way of life.

Superintendents and principals across the country who were interviewed for the *School Administration* article reported a wide variety of added duties, many of them considered temporary in nature in response to staff shortages and emergency needs. The theme seemed to echo an underlying admonition for rural administrators—and actually all administrators in general—a willingness to do what needs to be done.

Small school superintendents and principals have cleared snow from walkways, counseled college-bound students, taught special courses when others couldn't be found, supervised after-school programs, written a myriad of grants, chaperoned bus trips, painted buildings, and handled a wide variety of federal programs.

One was even called upon to corral a rattlesnake that had found its way onto the playground. She used a nearby garbage can to make the catch.

The demands in terms of time, energy, and talent are considerable in such assignments. But the experiences are rich and broad and for those interested in moving into positions of greater responsibility, successful experiences in such a position provide an excellent foundation in terms of on-the-job training.

A BROADER MENU OF RESPONSIBILITIES

A report entitled "Achieving Small School Success In Washington State," published jointly by the Office of the Superintendent of Public Instruction, the Washington Association of School Administrators, the Washington State School Directors Association, and the Rural Education Center at Washington State University, identified a number of challenges and courses of actions for administrators working in rural assignments.

Among its findings, the report indicated that most administrators working in small districts have no central office or specialist support to help prepare the myriad of required reports and complicated grant applications for critically-needed funding. Rules, regulations, paperwork, and mandatory reports for state and federal governments are the same for small and large districts regardless of staff size.

The report also acknowledges that small school administrators often face pressures that their large school counterparts do not experience; they perform under the microscope of community scrutiny; they control what may be the largest budget in town; and they are never "off duty."

This report reaffirms the need to seek outside support services and assistance such as education service districts—a concept which is explored in several different chapters.

The Washington study also reaffirms earlier comments about the value of small and rural school experiences as a background for movement into more expansive assignments. The study talks about recognition of the fact that small school leadership assignments should acknowledge the fact that success stories happen everywhere and that those who have begun their careers in smaller settings have multiple skills and abilities that are transferable to larger districts. Says the report, "student success stories happen everywhere and occur because someone developed a model, took a risk, or created an opportunity.

Such successes need to be shared and the models replicated in other areas. Where better to find new programs that work and people to lead them than in the crucible of small schools?"

Chapter One

Perpetuating Small Schools

Do the benefits of school consolidation outweigh the impact on local communities? Or is there any issue that can rally a small local community like the idea of losing its school? In the end, the real question is: As finances become tougher, will the residents in small communities be willing to pay the price and take the steps necessary to perpetuate their schools?

In the last 100 years or so, the number of school districts in America has dropped by as much as 90 percent. But despite this dramatic record of consolidation, the subject of merger among small districts continues to gain attention as states seek to balance their budgets in times of fiscal shortfalls.

In the wake of that threat, small school districts have circled the wagons in an effort to stave off the forces that would declare them obsolete and in need of merger.

In the course of that defense, many small districts have ignored efficiency and cost-cutting initiatives that might ultimately lead to their survival rather than their extinction. So fearful are they of their loss of identity and any moves toward cooperatives and contracted services that they have sometimes overlooked the very bold fiscal initiatives that might be critical to their solvency.

SAVING THE SCHOOL

While it might seem a bit political to openly discuss strategies for retaining small schools, there's really no point in discussing the entire gamut of survival skills for small school administrators without simultaneously creating a template for ensuring such schools are retained.

Part of being successful in small school administration is believing in the unique attributes they offer.

Survival in the small school principalship or superintendency is also as much about perpetuating the operation of the school as it is about a successful administrative experience. For the most part, the challenge involves devising ways to level the education playing field and making the most of limited financial and human resources.

In December of 1987, the Far West Educational Laboratory in San Francisco published a report from two Cornell researchers who suggested that small rural school districts might be better served by problem-solving options than by consolidation policies. They noted that it had been the long-time practice of the State of New York to simply consolidate small schools, when in fact, the problems that these school districts face are rarely just the consequence of their small size, hence they rarely will be solved by simply becoming larger.

They recommended a partial reorganization of school districts that includes more shared services and the use of distance learning and other telecommunication advancements. They suggest that rather than just talking consolidation, state officials ought to foster more dialogue about cooperation and sharing.

> Researcher Mary Anne Raywid, reporting in a 1999 *"ERIC Digest"*, stated that "qualitative studies have firmly established small schools as more productive and effective than larger ones."

The research tends to support the concept that small schools:

- offer more student participation opportunities;
- have fewer discipline problems;
- offer more meaningful adult connections;
- provide a safer school environment; and
- generally have lower class sizes.

In Oregon, during the 2009-2010 school year, there were 196 school districts. Of that number, 75 were under 500 students in enrollment, 106 were under 1,000 and 120 were under 1,500. There is no reason to believe these statistics wouldn't be fairly consistent across the country although the fact there are thirteen districts with fifteen or less pupils and 29 with less than 100 might be more likely to occur in large western states than in the east.

Nationally, although one-third of the children in America attend rural schools, policy makers tend to focus on the needs of urban and suburban districts. This is in part due to the fact that the impetus has been on consolidation and moving toward larger systems, not encouraging or perpetuating the existence or viability of smaller schools.

It is interesting then, in contrast, to note that the Gates Foundation has poured millions of dollars into states across the nation just to support its small schools initiatives suggesting there is a growing body of research which proves that smaller learning communities are typically more effective. Even major school systems such as Chicago, have made no secret of their desire to create smaller learning communities.

The Cornell study indicates that the idea there is a single optional school size or school district size is a myth that has played mischief in New York as well as other states. The source of the Cornell Study was found in *"Organizational Alternatives for Small Rural Schools: A Final Report to the New York State Legislature."*

Much of the focus of the Gates Foundation grants is working with larger schools. To date, not as much attention has been paid to schools which are small through no real choice of their own—most generally because they are isolated. These smaller schools would be well-advised to carefully follow the small schools movement and glean whatever information they can from this research project.

PRACTICAL THOUGHTS ABOUT SMALL SCHOOLS

Dan Morin, former superintendent of the North Douglas School District in Southwest Oregon, worried about the need to create stability in small districts. He noted that small districts are experiencing less and less flexibility as resources become tighter and that perhaps the answer for the perpetuation of small districts lies in creative alternatives that expand opportunities for students.

His colleague, Dave Gianotti, superintendent of the Riddle School District, about forty to fifty miles south of Drain, had previously worked at the Camas Valley Schools, high in the coast range between Roseburg and Coos Bay.

Said Gianotti, "in both Riddle and Camas Valley, the school is really all that is left in small areas like ours. People have made tremendous sacrifices, including, better paying job opportunities, to enjoy the benefits of a rural setting. Having made that sacrifice, they will do almost anything to find a way to keep their schools."

Gianotti is a proponent of the need to find ways to work with partners in order to expand services and opportunities for students. He is particularly active in working with regional agencies that can enhance the services in his district.

As funds have become tighter, Gianotti has found himself serving a dual role—as superintendent and as principal of the elementary school. It's no wonder he sees the superintendents and principals in small districts being stretched in many ways. With less staff, more demands, and fewer resources, the person in charge has to wear many hats

"We aren't alone in this," says Gianotti, "we have neighbors in the same boat. The key is to find ways to cooperate."

Before he moved to the Banks School District in Northwestern Oregon, Mark Jefferies worked as superintendent and the jack-of-all-trades in Paisley, a tiny outpost in Lake County, Oregon.

Jefferies was considered a leader among Oregon superintendents in terms of marshaling whatever resources he could find to keep Paisley afloat. He was a leader in the charter movement and in finding a variety of ways to do more with less.

Jefferies worried that as enrollment dropped and resources vanished, the core services of the district would become endangered. His charter school designation breathed new life into the district and the infusion of funding helped. "We were able to help make the future of the district more sustainable," said Jefferies, "and that has certainly helped them keep afloat."

Lake County, Oregon, where Paisley is located, is one of America's largest counties, so transportation to another district would be a major obstacle.

Before he became an elementary principal in Roseburg, Mike Kayser was superintendent of the Glide School District which has about 800 pupils.

Kayser is a strong believer in the importance of cooperatives. "Some cooperatives save 25 to 35 percent," he says, "and that makes a huge difference in the supply and materials budgets, whether it's a larger or a small district. In this day and age, administrators need to question a whole array of past practices in order to look at more cost-effective ways of doing business."

Until June of 2010, Dan Forbess served simultaneously as superintendent of the Oakland School District and the North Douglas School District which together have less than a thousand pupils. His dual role provided a daily reminder of the personal sacrifices he was making in order to help two districts handle the burden of leadership costs in the face of diminishing funding.

Forbess found himself overwhelmed by the external mandates being placed on districts in terms of both compliance and reporting. For that reason, he became a leader in finding creative solutions to the paperwork and minutiae associated with the job.

He is credited with having been the instigator of the Douglas County Special Education Leadership Consortium, which resulted in the creation of a cooperative administrative position serving five small districts.

North Lake is another district located in sparsely-populated Lake County. When that district began looking for a superintendent, they settled on Gordon Tope, a retired school leader who had served in Alaska overseeing a series of remote, scattered school sites.

Tope, who had moved to Arizona, flew to Oregon once a month to spend two weeks in the North Lake District. North Lake had experienced challenges in attracting high quality leadership and so they moved outside the traditional employment model when they contracted with Tope to oversee district management.

A beginning principal was employed by the district at the same time and he was mentored by Tope in order to provide for an effective leadership transition. This is an example of some of the challenges being faced by small districts as they seek to qualified individuals to fill the superintendent/principal role.

The Elkton School District is located along Highway 38 between Interstate 5 and Reedsport on the Oregon Coast. Their mascot is the elk, which says a great deal about their location in the Coast Range.

Rhonda Zoesel, now retired, said several years ago, "our district continues to be plagued with the decline in funding and increased demands placed on superintendents and principals and in particular those who wear both hats—which is most of us in small districts. We desperately need outside assistance from other agencies. Small schools need all kinds of support."

"One specific area where small districts need help is with policies," said Zoesel. "Perhaps a more uniform, regional approach might be the answer. Education is becoming extremely complex and without sophisticated help, it's hard to keep up. Most of all, small districts need things done for them, not to them. One such area would be grant-writing, which is a huge need for small schools."

Mike Hughes, who succeeded Zoesel at Elkton, has taken the district a step farther through several moves including charter status and the use of online courses to augment the curriculum. Under Hughes' leadership, enrollment in the district has increased by 35 percent and the district was named Oregon's fourteenth best high school. Earlier in the year it had been recognized as one of the best high schools in the nation.

Days Creek, with about 200 students, is located in the foothills of the Cascade Mountains and serves some of Oregon's most remote locations. Steve Chiavaro, a former superintendent, said "small schools need to consider contracting and sharing whenever possible. Historic small communities have deep, deep roots. Flexibility is becoming increasingly critical to districts. Our small district really is limited because of size, scope, capability, and resources."

Laurie Newton, who took the reins from Chiavaro, has leveraged the isolation, the poverty, and the unique nature of the Days Creek School District into a long line of special grants and sources of creative funding that has permitted the district to enjoy considerable enhancements and advancements.

Dick Wold, a long-time Oregon superintendent now retired to Pistol River in Curry County on the southern Oregon coast, was no stranger to small districts when he came to Riddle. He had already served as superintendent of the Sherman County School District in the wheat fields of Eastern Oregon.

Wold said "small school superintendents need to step out in positions of leadership. Too often, because of the myriad of demands which face them, they leave state and regional leadership activities to their colleagues from larger districts. When this happens, the voice of the small schools is not heard and we have a distinct message to share. We certainly have to be conscious of the need to be in our districts as much as possible, but when we do participate in selected events, we often bring back much more than we contribute.

The ESD can be an important source of collaboration and cooperation. Small districts need to negotiate various contracts with the ESD and other vendors which help them operate more effectively."

CREATING A NEW DISTRICT

For any superintendent who has sat back and wondered, "if I were creating a district from scratch, what would I change?" that very thing happened in Ione, Oregon.

In late 2002 or early 2003, a group of citizens in Ione, population 332, decided it was time to take the fate of their school district into their own hands. Ione had, for fifty years, been part of the Morrow County School District with a county-wide population of 2,400 students.

Due to declining enrollments in the southern part of the county and diminishing fiscal resources, there was talk of combining Ione High School with Heppner High School, eighteen miles to the south. The Ione Self-Determination Committee took their case to the Oregon Legislature and, much to the surprise of veteran Capital watchers, was granted permission to create a separate school district. Ione became only the second or third new district in Oregon in more than half a century since that state, like most others, had spent more than a century engaged in consolidation efforts.

Shortly after the Legislature gave Ione the green light, they were cut adrift from the Morrow County School District. Without a board of their own or any type of governance structure, they came under the guidance of the Umatilla-Morrow ESD. This took place in mid-June. The ESD superintendent became their superintendent in addition to his duties as superintendent of the ESD. By mid-July, a new five-member board was in place in Ione. The ESD superintendent remained as superintendent until July 1, 2004. As plans for the new school district were laid, leaders from the Ione community and the ESD had been involved in discussions about options for making the new district sustainable in the face of declining state funding.

> *In October of 2002, the Oregon Department of Education Office of School Finance, Data, and Analysis, produced a report on the costs of operating small schools in Oregon. Commissioned by Interim Legislative Committees on Education, the report was designed to provide both an analysis of the costs of operating small schools and suggestions for more efficient practices.*
>
> *That report advised that strategies should be developed with ESDs to increase the efficiency of operating small schools. The report also suggested that spreading fixed costs more effectively through the use of an ESD model might be one answer. The report also specifically pointed to large-group purchasing of supplies, equipment, and services as another potential model for cost savings. All of these suggestions were incorporated into the Ione Model—and subsequent models which have now been expanded to other districts across the State of Oregon.*

As John Rietmann, one of the founding members of the Ione Board, but now retired, stated at the time, "we want to become a model for how small, rural districts can survive. We have the unique opportunity of building our district from the ground up and we can structure that process around finding ways to do business differently."

Seven years after the Ione project was undertaken, a special task force appointed by the governor has made similar recommendations for adoption across the state.

One of the first changes in Ione was to turn to the ESD for management services in literally every area except actual classroom instruction. During the 2003-2004 school year the district even contracted for a superintendent although they maintained a site administrator. In 2004-2005 they employed a superintendent/principal although the ESD continued to provide some level of mentorship and management oversight. In the fall of 2010, they returned to the idea of contracting with the ESD for a superintendent and retaining a site administrator.

Some of the areas of contracting have included:

- The district has no deputy clerk—all business functions including payroll are handled by the ESD—the site administrator and building secretary code purchase orders and send them on the ESD. Most regular bills, such as utilities, go directly to the ESD—as does the basic revenue.
- The ESD is the personnel office for Ione, including recruitment, selection, contract management, and negotiations.
- The ESD manages all technology functions.
- The ESD contracts for food service and maintenance/custodial.
- The district contracts with a private carrier for transportation.
- The ESD provides all curriculum, testing and assessment, and staff development services.
- The ESD Special Education director also serves in the same capacity for Ione.
- The ESD provides printing and purchasing services.
- Ione has an administrator who, along with the teaching staff, handles daily operations including, of course, instruction.
- A multi-million dollar building project was underway when the district was formed and the ESD contracted for oversight services in order to assure the project was completed properly.
- The district contracted with the City of Ione to mow and water its athletic field. The city had purchased a new $30,000 mower which it used for the task. The school district did not own any mowing equipment. The city charged $30 per hour for the job and was able to help amortize its purchase. The district does not have to bear the cost of purchasing the equipment, maintaining the equipment, or paying someone to operate it.
- In the fall of 2004, the District was faced with a $50,000 drainage problem. A work party was organized and more than forty local residents showed up for two days with an armada of equipment and a strong interest in saving money. The project was completed for less than $5,000.
- The district ran a bond issue to update the high school and expand the elementary school and considered the idea of spending as much as $500,000 for a weight room. Instead, the district contracted with a private individual to rent a former hardware store several blocks away for $400. The weight room/fitness center is used by students and the community.

Because of its limited staff, the Ione Board has formed two major committees—the Buildings & Grounds Committee, which oversees maintenance as well as long-range needs, and the Student Success Committee, which deals with a variety of ways to expand services to students and improve both staff development and student achievement.

The work of the Building & Grounds Committee is outlined in more detail in Chapter 12.

While the district cannot afford the services of a counselor, it contracted with a specialist who comes one day a week to work with students having behavior issues. Other counseling duties such as helping students schedule themselves or prepare for college are handled by the Student Success Committee. This committee often calls upon recent graduates to assist students with their transition to higher education and to meet with younger students to provide guidance in early course selection.

The district does not have a licensed media specialist but has contracted for fifteen days of service from a professional, licensed individual who oversees media practices.

In the Ione model, the staff was reduced by three teaching periods in order to create revenues for on-line instruction. The fiscal value of the three teaching periods was more than enough to cover the costs of all on-line courses which might be needed by students. Aides at the school are being used for monitoring the on-line learning.

The Ione Education Foundation, a separate community entity, was created to provide support to the school system. The Foundation tries to focus its contributions on enhancements and special grants such as field trips, professional growth, and other enrichment activities. The Foundation has funded a half-time music instructor and a primary position to avoid operating combined classes.

COOPERATIVES AND CONTRACTS

There generally isn't a great deal of concern over who pays the bills or handles the myriad of other details surrounding the management of a school district. People mostly care who is teaching their children and what they are being taught. And in such communities, they want to retain their identity by offering their children the opportunity to participate in a wide variety of extra-curricular activities. All of these interests can be addressed by the local board.

It is possible to achieve considerable savings while retaining local identity and control.

It is likely there will be mounting pressure for small districts to both consider consolidation and to consider contracting out for services such as business, human resources, food service, special education, transportation, and other operational functions to larger organizations.

This pressure is the product of a budget crisis that has gripped America's schools. While the research on whether or not consolidation even provides for greater efficiency is inconclusive, the pressure continues. In return, despite their economic challenges, many districts are strongly averse to the idea of relinquishing any of the functions they have normally conducted in part because of concern it could lead to consolidation.

Communities which house small schools would be well-advised to look seriously at those ventures which might ultimately provide the resources to keep teachers in the classrooms even if there are community concerns that such cooperative ventures might be misunderstood as steps toward a merger.

Chapter Two

Getting (And Keeping) The Job: The Transition From Training To Employment

The process of "getting the job" really begins when an individual enters the field of education. Since first impressions are lasting impressions, would-be administrators would be well-advised to remember that the creation of a reputation begins on Day One of their career. An assistant principal, who used to leave minutes after the students had left the building was asked about his schedule. He noted "once I become a principal I will work longer hours." A good work ethic isn't something folks turn on and off. It is embedded in practice.

Candidates entering the pipeline need to do everything possible to get involved in the operation of the school—special projects, committees, and most things the principal doesn't want to do. Basically, they need to become essential and a natural for a job when it opens. With the decline in revenues and cutbacks in help for superintendents and principals, there are plenty of growth opportunities available for aspiring and ambitious candidates.

Take advantage of opportunities to experience new responsibilities and to participate in regional events, which involve administrators. Get to know the people at the education service district. Become visible in the community and attend as many school events as possible.

Once the internship has been completed, it's a good idea to remain involved rather than pocketing the certificate and returning to life as it looked before the training program began. Besides, in many schools or districts, fellow staff members begin to treat aspiring administrators "just a little bit differently" once it becomes known they are upwardly mobile and it is hard to go back anyway. By staying involved, candidates provide constant reminders of their interest in potential openings.

Even after extensive preparation, there are candidates who are reluctant to venture forth and throw their hat in the ring. One prospective school administrator had the following saying posted clearly on the wall as a reminder of the importance of taking the initial plunge. It is good advice: "*A ship is safest in the harbor, but that's not what it was built for.*"

LOCATING THE OPENINGS

Just a few short years ago, who would have thought that almost any administrative job would literally become a national search even if the district has no desire to seek applicants far and wide? In the age of the Internet, candidates can locate job openings through a variety of search engines.

Originally, the primary source of administrative job postings was through college and university placement services. While those outlets still offer information about potential jobs, they are playing a much less significant role as the primary source of postings for key leadership positions.

The new sources of information are state school boards associations, state administration associations, and printed and on-line postings from search consultants. Another major player in the field is *Education Week*, which carries an extensive classified section—particularly during hiring season. There are also a number of private Web sites such as EdZapp and similar outlets.

The available sources of postings changes almost daily due to accessibility to the Internet. Many candidates go on-line and simply type in key words related to job procurement in order to find new Web sites.

CONTACTING A CONSULTANT

Many individuals who are interested in relocation develop contacts with one or more search consultants. Through such a contact they are able to make the consultant familiar with their geographical interests and as well as the particulars in terms of school district size and position.

Candidates should take the time to visit with influential school leaders such as ESD superintendents or association executives about being interested in administration. They often hear of opportunities and can put candidates in touch when the right position comes along.

BEING KIND TO THE SECRETARY

First impressions are lasting. The initial contact with a district will rarely be with the superintendent, the consultant, or the board chair. It will most likely be with a secretary. When applying for an administrative position and talking to the receptionist, administrative assistant, or deputy clerk, candidates should remember that person is starting to weigh the merits of a potential new boss. It's very likely that those opinions will be shared with those making the final decision.

More than once when screening for principal candidates, secretaries have subtly assured that the files of candidates with whom they have had positive contact somehow seem to get a disproportionate look while the files of those who are rude and demeaning somehow end up on the bottom of the pile.

School administrators in the process of interviewing teachers have sometimes been known to make sure that candidates had five or ten minutes to sit outside the interview room in a position to have casual contact with the secretary to the principal. The reports of that contact were often as valid (or more valid) than the results of the interview process.

> *One such example of the importance of this concept came during a round of interviews at a small, central Oregon district. While the board and district business manager were conducting the four interviews, the district secretary was outside greeting the candidates and handling the interview details. Following the interviews, the board gathered to make its final decision. During that time, they became aware of which candidate did not make eye contact with the secretary during a conversation, which candidate helped the secretary unload dinner from her car and help carry the dinner into the district office, which candidate virtually ignored the secretary, which candidate used the time they were waiting for the interview to learn more about the district, including the secretary's impressions as parent and employee, and which candidate didn't even bother to say goodbye to the secretary when leaving.*

MATERIALS

Most jobs ask for some basics from a candidate. In the case of Northwest Leadership Associates, those basics generally include a completed application, a letter of application, four or more current letters of recommendation (or possibly a university placement file), and a resume. Nothing else.

Some districts may want a philosophy of education or a specific response to certain challenges and issues, which they have put forth. Most want that included in the letter of application.

The longest application Northwest Leadership ever received included 361 pages of material—including magazine articles, various curriculum papers, photocopies of certificates, etc. The best applications ever received have been responsive to the information requested by the board. Although candidates often bring videos or cd's, teams almost never stop to view those materials or adjourn to spend time poring over a three-ring binder. Candidates should come to the interview with a notebook on which to write possible questions or notations. Not much else is needed.

When presentations of candidate files are being made to boards or superintendents (most principalship searches involve presentations to the superintendent) the time allotted is generally in the neighborhood of two hours or less. In larger districts, that has extended to as much as six or eight hours—but that is the exception, not the rule. Two to three hours is standard.

Candidates should consider the fact the consultants are bringing anywhere from a dozen to three dozens files to a board for their consideration. The consultant and board are also using that same time space to finalize questions, frame the interview process, and handle other details. A two-hour session provides 120 minutes, a three-hour session means 180 minutes. If there are 12 files and two hours, that's ten minutes per file. And, lots of other things happen during that two hours. With more files, the minutes begin to diminish. Consultants have all the time they want to dig through files in meticulous detail—boards do not.

It is a good idea for candidates to bounce the file off a spouse or a professional friend. How much of it can they read in ten minutes or less? If they can't read it in the allotted time, they shouldn't expect someone else to do so. This doesn't mean that boards don't come back and spend more time taking files home and reviewing them in depth. But, first impressions are critical and it makes no sense to obliterate the most important data in the interest of adding bulk.

Also, when preparing the resume, it is important not to obscure watershed achievements by burying them in the depths of mundane professional outings.

In most cases, materials will need to be reproduced to share with each board member or the selection committee. Candidates should provide an application format that is compatible with that process, including making sure what is provided will copy advantageously, and also, making sure the application materials can be broken apart readily for reproduction.

MAILING

Sometimes elaborate mailing efforts can create more problems than they solve. Most reputable carriers can deliver parcels in a timely manner—without the need for signatures. The cost, as of this printing, is about $4.85 for priority mail. Other charges differ with the carrier. Actually, regular mail isn't a bad option, either. Elaborate, last-minute mailings which might cost $15-$25 are mostly a pain to consultants who generally have to chase around town to a local FedEx or UPS Office or the post office to sign for and receive the materials.

In addition, most searches provide about six weeks of lead time. Neither the consultant nor the board are impressed if candidates master the art of having their applications magically arrive on the final date. A week or two early often provides for a more thorough review of both the materials and the ability to contact references in a timely manner.

People involved with the selection process begin asking a week or two in advance of the deadline date if there are applications and if they can begin looking them over.

If a candidate wants to turn in the materials at the last possible minute it important to remember the turn-around time before the consultant meets with the board may be a matter of days. Since it is not unusual for consultants to spend a week or more trying to make contact with references this limits the amount of information the consultant can secure. Wise candidates get their materials in soon enough to contribute to the convenience of the consultant and others involved in securing references.

RESUMES

For the most part, resumes are too long!! Veteran candidates might have longer resumes because they have more to say. Fledgling candidates just need to accept the limitations of their experiences and not try to overkill. Most boards are looking for some key experiences or contributions to public education.

There is a wonderful old saying called "Less Is More." If a candidate has been president of the regional principals association or been involved in some professional assignment that required many hours of commitment, such information shouldn't be buried between attendance at a half-day workshop and service on a committee that met twice for a total of five hours. Candidates should spotlight major achievements and not obscure them in the interest of volume.

Chapter 2
VISITATIONS

It is disappointing how few candidates actually visit a district in which they are interested and how many boards are prone to remark, "it's amazing to know that they are expecting us to pay them a $100,000 or more to do this job and they don't care enough to come look us over or learn more about us."

One candidate interested in a principalship said he wanted additional information about a district so he drove 140 miles to the district to spend the night and look around in his desire to learn more about the opening. He sprang for a motel and the gas. He liked what he saw and wanted to know more. Based upon conversations with boards, they like the fact he had cared enough to visit. He, like others who invest in the process, was provided every ounce of information and time he demanded.

Because of advances in technology and the use of the Internet, it isn't particularly difficult to access Web sites that have student achievement information, demographic information, budget data, and a host of other facts and figures. Being able to weave real facts into application materials and the interview demonstrates that the candidate is genuinely interested in the district.

It's equally surprising when a candidate calls and says "I'm interested in the Fairview, Oregon School District—where is it?" If the candidate isn't willing to spend two minutes on the Internet searching for the location, it is reasonable to believe they aren't going to be particularly energetic or thorough in any other aspect of the process either.

Candidates should try to get a feel for the particular nature of the community. Several years ago, a candidate for a position in a small, rural district of 230 students arrived in town a day early. This is a lumber town with a few scattered ranches thrown in for good measure. One of his first acts was to visit the elementary school and advise the teachers that they could expect larger class sizes the following year.

Perhaps even more notable was the fact that as the board president walked the candidate out to his car following the formal interview, he noticed that the candidate had a very large "Earth First" sticker attached to his bumper. This is not intended to be a political assessment of the philosophies of any group—only a suggestion that such a position would be a hard sell to a board made up of individuals who depend upon logging and grazing for their livelihood.

In another recent search process, a young principal and his family drove 250 miles to spend several days in a prospective district. That effort did not go unnoticed by a board that might not have otherwise considered his candidacy. It is amazing how little time and effort some candidates will invest in both learning more about a district where they hope to take charge of the community's most valuable asset and where they, themselves, might want to establish a home.

Again and again, search consultants see seasoned veterans outdistanced by eager new candidates who have invested time in learning the basics about a district.

DRESS

It is a generally-accepted principle that candidates will look the best they ever will on the day of the interview. They might someday be able to afford better clothes, but the nature of the dress is a solid indicator. While dress styles have relaxed considerably in recent years, there are still few interview situations in which anything less than a coat and tie for men and a dress suit or dress for a woman are considered acceptable in a formal interview for an administrative position.

Candidates wishing to make a fashion statement, might wish to choose another venue for that activity. Neutral colors or clothing are always a safe bet saving the wild tie, the massive earrings, or similar penchants for another time. One candidate wore a tie in the school colors of a small district and this act gained positive attention from several board members.

THE INTERVIEW

Candidates should give some serious thought to the critical elements which should be included in the brief overview of training, experience, and qualifications. Generally, about five minutes is provided for this overview. It's a good idea to make sure that the vital pieces are incorporated and that advance attention has been given to the basics of this portion of the interview process.

In many districts, particularly with final interviews, candidates may have the opportunity to meet with a variety of different groups. In some cases, "observers" might travel along to help provide introductions and assure that the process works well. They will also be wanting to make sure that there are consistencies in answers between groups.

Even if there aren't "observers" or hosts, people might well compare notes. Rather than succumbing to the temptation to tell each group what they want to hear, candidates are better served to be sure an element of consistency is incorporated.

It is also important to thoroughly review the materials about the job regarding the challenges, qualifications, and qualities suggested for the candidate and identify four to five items that must be included regardless of the questions. These issues should be covered over and over before the interview so that it becomes natural to weave them into the interview process. The four or five items for inclusion would be experiences, concepts, or thoughts that are particularly defining in terms of a candidacy.

Qualified candidates making a comprehensive review of the requirements of a position ought to be able to quickly identify those specific items in their background that should help separate them from the balance of the field. It is important to assure that the interview team becomes aware of these items.

There is no such thing as a generic job interview. Often, in working with districts, consultants have the opportunity to meet and greet candidates as they arrive for interviews. Typically, they ask if there are specific questions about the nature of the board, what they are like, what the consultants have discovered in working with the district during the search process, and so forth.

Some candidates ask precise and well-planned questions designed to further help them prepare for their meeting with the board. Others are rather casual in their approach, suggesting that they are journey-level candidates who have been to more than a few rodeos in their past—sort of an "if you have seen one district, you have seen them all" approach.

Several years ago, a larger school district attracted a celebrated field of candidates. One such celebrity candidate arrived about ten minutes early and was offered answers to any questions the candidate might have. This happened to be a person who had initially been projected as the leader in the clubhouse. The candidate indicated that "he just wanted to be himself….what they see is what they get. If the board gets serious, I'll do more homework."

In the course of two days, the board conducted six preliminary interviews and selected three finalists. Absent from that list were individuals with some incredibly impressive resumes. In their place were candidates who had clearly done their homework about the district and took the time to tailor their presentations and responses to the materials provided in advance by the district.

Candidates should not use the interview as an opportunity to critically assess the district. While the board will ultimately want some problems solved, the interview process isn't a place for a management review of current operations. It is a bit presumptive to use this occasion to provide the board with insights into their dirty laundry and how it could be cleaned.

"DO YOU HAVE ANY QUESTIONS?"

At the end of most interviews, the team will ask the candidate if they have any questions of their own. It is primarily a courtesy and by that point in the interview, most participants are ready for a break. This is a time when the route to take is a few well-planned questions mostly designed to make a positive impression.

This is not the time to ask about pay, benefits, length of contract, and other employment-related issues. Those answers can be provided by the consultant, by studying salary reports, or through other sources, including on occasion, the previous principal or superintendent. A couple of good questions that make a positive impression might include:

- How do you feel about professional development for your administrators? What opportunities are provided for their growth?
- If this were June of next year and if I had been your principal during the past year, what two or three things would you most like for me to have accomplished in my initial year?
- What do you want in terms of board-superintendent communication?
- If you were to identify the things about this district of which you are the most proud, what would they be?

REALISTIC APPLICATION EFFORTS

Not long ago a search firm received a five-page application letter from a candidate for a fairly good opening. The first page had been modified to reflect the specific opening for which the candidate was applying. The remaining four pages were clearly boilerplate which had been copied from previous applications. While the candidate pool is lower than it has been in the past, it isn't so low that districts don't take the time to determine if the candidate is involved in mass applications or has a genuine interest in a specific position.

Candidates should carefully choose potential job openings that make sense and spend time putting together a quality product to submit with those applications. If it becomes necessary to just send out generic materials, a candidate's list is too long.

Before beginning the application process, prospective candidates would be well-served to develop a realistic measure of their prospective candidacy. Consultants can certainly be called upon to provide that advice. It is also important to realize that an individual might be an attractive candidate in one situation and not as attractive in another based upon specific skills. In most job postings, the district takes the time to identify those characteristics of the district and the expectations of candidates. Candidates should compare their education and experience as well as personal strengths with the district criteria.

Word ultimately gets out about who is applying where. Too many unrealistic applications and the seriousness of one's candidacy begins to slip. While there are rare examples of someone moving from a principalship to a major superintendency, those examples are few and far between.

Likewise, a high school of 1,200 students probably won't consider a principal who is coming directly from the classroom in contrast to candidates who have either served as an assistant principal in a large high school or as principal of a mid-sized school. Entry-level candidates are well-advised to familiarize themselves with entry-level positions.

It never hurts to ask the advice of those you respect and trust. The purpose of that process, however, is to solicit their advice, not to convince them of something else.

IF YOU GET THE JOB

Administrators interviewing beginning teachers sometimes ask the candidates to describe what they would do on the first day. Occasionally, a candidate responds with "you know, I really haven't thought about it." Since they had completed their training and were on the job market, it would seem like the time had come to give that subject some serious thought.

Ironically, this story has a relationship to what is sometimes found with superintendents or principals who are offered jobs. Even though they have spent countless hours preparing application materials, have often visited the community, are aware of the job demands and the proposed compensation, and have gone through the interview process, they haven't given serious thought to what they would do if a proposal is made.

Particularly in the case of superintendencies, boards will invest considerable time and energy in the selection process. Following the interview process, and often on the final day of the interviews, the board will meet to make a decision. If it's not too late at night, the assembled board will enthusiastically place a call to their first choice to offer the job. Hopefully they will receive an equally enthusiastic and immediate acceptance, but not always. Some other responses include:

- "Could I have a few days to talk this over and get some advice from my colleagues?"

- "This is good news. Could I call back tomorrow after I have had a chance to talk with my wife and family to see how they feel?"
- "I realize you indicated in the brochure that you were willing to pay $75,000 but to be honest, I won't come for less than $80,000."
- "If you don't mind, I would like to sleep on it."
- "I've thought about the job and while I am flattered you would offer it to me, I had already decided not to take it if it was offered."
- Or, sometimes candidates will visit with their families and decide to decline once the offer has been made.

In is important for candidates to bear in mind that the board wishes to hire a leader and chief decision maker and this is the first example provided them in terms of what they might expect. Don't be surprised if they are suddenly deflated. And, search consultants don't particularly like "helping candidates to the altar" and then getting jilted at the last moment anymore than districts do. A second chance won't come so easily.

In a recent search the candidate indicated he would like to be called no matter how late the decision-making meeting took place. When the board chair finally called, (about 10:30 p.m.) in the presence of other board members, he was greeted by an answering machine.

Candidates should carefully consider in advance the possibility of being offered the job whether it is a principalship or a superintendency. They should consider and plan their response when the call comes. In most cases the salary has been made known which takes care of that question in advance. The potential employers will also assume—and rightly so—that candidates will have dealt with family issues in advance. A child doesn't instantly become poised to enter their senior year sometime between the interview and the job offer. A spouse rarely makes new career decisions of their own during the same time period.

The board will assume the candidate collaborated with colleagues and/or family in advance of making application and certainly by the time the interview process is completed. The board will also assume if there was a decision not take the job even if was offered following the interview or a district visit, the candidate will have called or written to withdraw.

In short, candidates need to do their homework and be prepared to be responsive to an offer. Boards and other hiring officials aren't impressed that candidates aren't as fully committed to the marriage as they are and that some doubts might persist. Getting off on the right foot is critical and while it might not seem like a big thing, the simple act of responding to the job offer is a vital part of the first impression.

Furthermore, board members are volunteers and busy people who don't like to waste their time interviewing candidates who aren't serious about the job. They are also not impressed by candidates who use the application process to secure a salary increase or some other contractual benefit in their current assignment. Or, simply want to get involved in a superintendent or principal search for some other self-serving reason apart from being a serious candidate.

IN CASE SOMEONE ELSE GETS THE JOB

"When things go your way we learn a little about you. When things don't go your way, we learn a lot about you."

Since it is quite possible that a candidate may not get the first job he or she apply for, it is almost as important to address what to do if one doesn't get the job as if one does. More than one unsuccessful candidate for a position has impaired a career by approaching defeat in an unprofessional manner. If the candidate is going to call and seek information about the decision, it is vital to simply listen carefully rather than arguing about a decision that has already been made.

After one recent search, a call was made to each of the finalists to let them know what had happened. One of the candidates launched into a rather lengthy assessment of the other four finalists including an assessment of the individual who had been selected.

Since such calls are always a difficult part of a search, the consultant listened politely while the candidate explained the considerable frustration about the process and the competition. Another candidate complimented the process and expressed appreciation for having been included and considered. Still another candidate primarily focused on having enjoyed the process and expressed a continuing desire to be considered for other openings. The other candidate primarily followed this same format indicating she appreciated the call, suspected it was never easy, noted she was disappointed, and graciously asked that the consultants express her thanks to the district. Any of the latter three will probably get more chances at other openings.

In some cases, spouses or even parents have called to express outrage or to demand to know why their candidate had been overlooked. Consultants or districts are reluctant to put themselves in harm's way a second time by advancing people whose involvement in a search might promote such actions.

Several years ago, a well-qualified assistant superintendent was interested in moving into a superintendency. He applied for a district with 1,600 students and one with more than 3,000 students in his first effort. For various reasons, he didn't get selected as one of the four individuals who interviewed in the smaller district. He did get a preliminary interview in the 3,000-student district but didn't make it into the finals. His next effort was a 4,000-student district where he almost instantly became the front-runner. He served very successfully in that district for ten years.

There were two lessons to be learned from this situation. The first is the fact that he didn't burn any bridges after the first two unsuccessful attempts. The second is that it is sometimes rather difficult to predict who will be the perfect fit. In fact, many consultants are able to play a key role in helping the board identify the finalists, but after that, it is often chemistry that plays a bigger role than any other factors. This candidate was apparently not a good fit in the first two districts, but an ideal fit for the third.

Two of the individuals who have the greatest challenge in maintaining a happy face in the wake of a negative decision are assistant superintendents seeking an in-house superintendency or assistant principals seeking to move up in the same building. In both cases, they most likely have a supportive constituency anxious to engage in getting after the decision makers for not choosing their candidate.

A former in-house candidate for the job of superintendent related this story. "During the weekend the board was making its decision, a sage retiree who happened to be visiting in the area called and asked if the board had selected anyone. He noted the importance of being prepared for the possibility that it could be a no vote and that this would be an incredibly difficult time suggesting that lots of people would be watching to see how the losing candidate reacted and many of them would want to make a scene.

He also cited examples of others in the same boat that had become outspoken and then, as they began working for the new superintendent, actually were disloyal and undermined the new leader. While it may have provided some immediate satisfaction, several of those individuals spent years trying to get positions elsewhere. Their unprofessional conduct had undermined their credibility and their upward mobility."

In the end, the candidate did get the no vote and the scenario unfolded exactly as promised. The candidate had to take a very deep breath and swallow his pride. The best friends at this point are those who provide comfort and support without seeking to perpetuate anything negative. In this case, one even suggested that for everything there is a reason and that there must be something better down the road. In retrospect, there was and the candidate moved on to an even better position.

Chapter 2
KEEPING THE JOB

There will certainly be many points in this book when issues related to keeping the job will be touched upon. One of the most important considerations in this regard is being able to develop work priorities. Work priorities means deciding what is important and giving consideration to requests and directives which come from above whether it is the board or the superintendent.

Sometimes administrators feel it is all right to ignore the requests of superiors because they "have too much on their plate" or are "busy with other matters." As a rule of thumb, it's a good practice to consistently be responsive to requests from above remembering most boards and superintendents don't ask principals to do things that they don't want done.

Or, in the words of Walt Hanline, a former superintendent of the year in California and now a successful consultant, "we have the time to do anything we want, we just don't have the time to do everything we want." He also extends his thoughts to budgets and makes equal sense when he says "in most cases we have sufficient funds in the budget to do anything we want, we just don't have enough money to do everything."

It has always been interesting to observe that on one end of the spectrum there are people who are able to manage the world's largest corporations and make it appear relatively easy. On the other, there are those who are barely able to handle the demands of their daily lives without becoming overwhelmed by the responsibility and sheer magnitude of the project.

The latter would probably include those people who remind colleagues at about Thanksgiving time that they won't be available until January "because they are too busy getting ready for Christmas." This group would also include the martyrs who create a mantle of self-importance by reminding anyone and everyone just how busy they are.

Leadership is, among other things, about "getting a grip." If someone's plate is too full in their present job or if they appear overwhelmed by their current assignment, it suggests perhaps they can't handle their current duties and may not be a good candidate for something more responsible.

Martyrdom may have a place, but this isn't it.

Chapter Three

Creating An Entry Plan

"People don't care how much you know until they know how much you care."

The idea of an "entry plan" might conjure up the vision of a new educational leader parading into town with school children tossing rose petals along the way and the high school band playing "Hail To The Chief." Unfortunately, a realistic and effective entry plan is far less dramatic, but no less important.

First impressions are lasting impressions, and what the superintendent or principal does during those critical first days and months will play a pivotal role in charting future success and can lay the groundwork for a successful tour of duty. A properly-executed entry plan will also lay the foundation for converting the expectations established during the selection process into genuine action plans.

One new administrator arrived on the job and in good faith decided that it would be important to get to know key staff members and initiate dialogue. He had his secretary send out the following message.

> *"I'm here and anxious for you to be able to meet me. Please call and schedule an appointment as soon as possible so that I can share my ideas for the future of the district with you."*

A second administrator in another district made personal telephone calls to the key staff members asking if there was a time when she could come visit their building/work site/classroom and have a chance to meet them in person, to which she added, "I would like to have a tour of your area and have you tell me what you think I ought to be focusing on." Another, knowing staff members were on summer vacation, volunteered to come visit in their homes if that would be easier.

The reception and the initial impressions were predictable. One got off to a good start while the other managed to annoy his new colleagues before he even got out of the starting gate.

BEFORE ARRIVING

Often there is a hiatus between the time that the new administrator is chosen and when that person arrives on the job. One new superintendent actually conducted a very deliberate interview process prior to arriving in order to identify common themes and use the results as a starting point for understanding areas for future attention.

The interview process, which can be conducted in person or by telephone can involve board members, other administrators, staff, students, and community leaders. In the case noted above, a total of thirty-five individuals were involved.

The process of what questions to ask was carefully considered. Rather than just using open-ended questions that asked "how do you feel about your schools?" or "are you satisfied with the level of student expectations?" the new administrator used the effective schools research to build the questions. These criteria for effective schools helped provide a more systematic approach to gaining understanding. In this instance, the new superintendent visited the district and met each of the prospective interviewees for the purpose of a face-to-face meeting and a chance to explain the process.

The actual interviews took thirty to sixty minutes and were conducted by phone from his previous location in another state. The interviews were taped so that he could identify recurring themes. Once the data was gathered, it became the basis for the district's visioning process. The results were much more specific and identifiable rather than being generalized.

In many search processes, time is spent working with stakeholders to identify the qualities and qualifications of a candidate as well as the challenges facing the district. These criteria can also be used as an effective framework for conducting the entry survey. In both examples, the process is marked by a thoughtful and thorough approach and speaks to the importance of seeing matters through fresh eyes and an objective capacity to determine a readiness for change.

While the process noted above was conducted by a superintendent, it is easily transportable to the principalship and fact, in the same district where the superintendent conducted the process noted earlier, a new high school principal had just been chosen. He was encouraged to conduct a survey of his own as part of the entry plan.

There were several by-products of the entry effort implemented in this situation in that the new superintendent was able to model several important leadership traits including listening skills, an interest in data-driven decision making, and a willingness to collaborate with stakeholders to identify problems—all of which took place before he even stepped into his office for the first time.

> One new ESD superintendent visited each of the fifty schools served by the agency and met with as many staff members as he could. He asked them three informal questions—"who do you know from the ESD?" "when was the last time you saw them?" and "what did they do for you?" The themes that emerged from these questions framed the basis for helping provide a new direction for the ESD which included a significantly enhanced level of visibility with regular classroom teachers in terms of both programs and services.

WHOM TO TRUST

One of the initial challenges in a new administrative job will be determining whom to trust. It is reasonably safe to assume that there will be situations when it will be necessary to gain the advice of others. Anyone who has been a new student knows that the first kids who come forward aren't necessarily the ones an individual will want to have as friends down the line.

This is often the case in new administrative jobs as well. Some individuals will immediately begin jockeying for position as insiders.

A good practice is to remain neutral and listen to all sides and gradually began to identify patterns. It is particularly important to maintain a neutral posture with the board and provide equal access and equal, consistent flows of information.

> A veteran school administrator talks about taking his first principalship and being given one piece of advice by the superintendent: the names of a couple of influential teachers in the building who formed the "power base." The superintendent suggested that the principal might want to bounce his ideas off of those individuals before surfacing them. It was not a plan designed to make the principal ineffective, but rather it was designed to help the principal gain an understanding of any objections or issues which might arise with a new proposal—in advance. After the first year, he found that while he still remained in communication, he was doing a lot less checking.
> At the same time, during the initial stages of getting his feet on the ground, the veteran staff members had been an invaluable resource.

NEW ADMINISTRATORS WORKSHOP

In most states, including Oregon and Washington, state professional organizations conduct a new administrators workshop. This should be considered a must if at all possible. This is a chance to meet state leaders from the school boards association, school administrators, professional licensing, and the department of education as well as others who are new to administrative positions in the state. They often become valuable networking contacts.

VISITING CLASSROOMS AND WORK SITES

"If you roll up your sleeves, you are less likely to lose your shirt."

Once classes get underway, it's a good idea to make it a priority to visit teachers and aides in their classrooms. It is also important to make it a point to visit the kitchens, boiler rooms, bus garage, offices, and wherever else employees are on the job. The first visit may well come as a surprise if the staff aren't used to having their administrators out and about. The second, third, fourth, and fifth visits will cement the idea that this is an administrator who intends to be visible and word will soon spread.

For various reasons, administrators find it easier to schedule themselves out of the district for an entire day or days to attend conferences and training sessions. It is much more difficult to schedule an entire day devoted to visiting students and staff within the district even though the latter practice generally pays more dividends.

Once a pattern of visibility develops, staff members are less likely to schedule appointments in the principal's office or at the district office because they know they will soon see that person wandering about. Often, the questions they have can be handled quickly without time-consuming appointments.

As a rule, administrators need to check their calendars very carefully to assure that they are spending more time *out in* their building or their district than they are *out of* their building or their district.

In conducting searches for administrative positions, the consultant generally meets with staff, community members, boards, and others to solicit input about the qualities and qualifications of the new person and the challenges he or she might face. Almost without exception, the leading issue is finding an administrator who will be visible in the classrooms, is comfortable being around students, regularly attends school events, and takes part in community affairs. If the person does that alone once they are on the job, it is likely he or she will have laid the foundation for success.

Administrators need to literally become fanatical about the importance of being in classrooms and in schools. If such a pattern is put into place at the outset, it becomes a routine.

At the Umatilla-Morrow ESD, there is a large sign painted over the entryway that reminds employees "if you are here, you aren't there." Obviously there are some staff members at an education service agency or in a district office whose jobs are such they need to remain behind their desk. But it's well to remember there are seldom, if ever, students in the ESD office or the school district office and the more time staff spend in the field, the better.

DOING SOMETHING THAT VISIBLY MAKES A DIFFERENCE

A new superintendent in one Eastern Oregon district noticed that the reception area in the district office was dirty and probably hadn't been painted in forty years. The secretaries told him early on that it was an embarrassment and they wished they could do something about it but they also knew that there was no money in the budget to have it painted. Also, if they did spend money on it, there might be a backlash about using district dollars to dress-up the "head shed."

Someone got the idea if all they had to do was buy the paint, the expense would be minimal. One weekend, the superintendent, the secretaries, and some willing family members came to the office in old clothes and painted it themselves. There was anything but a backlash from the staff. Instead, there was a universal impression that the new leader wasn't afraid to roll up his sleeves and get the job done, even if money was short. And the secretaries proudly showed off their gleaming new surroundings to anyone who came near.

In another district, which had been ripped with controversy surrounding the previous superintendent and related issues, the head football coach took it upon himself to find a way to do something positive to help put things back on track.

It so happened that the district had a reasonably—good stadium, but it had fallen into disrepair and was weed-infested. The coach came to visit the new superintendent, who had been on the job about a week, and shared his idea. He said it would be a good project but only if the new superintendent were willing to come. The following Saturday, the new administrator arrived at the stadium with a weed-eater in hand, dressed in old blue jeans and a tee shirt, wearing the new Mustang hat the coach had provided.

The football team was there along with their parents, the members of the Booster Club, an assortment of local citizens, student leaders, and anyone else who was willing to help. The group worked for five hours and then stopped for a hamburger feed during which everyone had a chance to get to know each other a little better. A skeleton crew remained in the afternoon to load up the debris and haul it away. The new superintendent even filled his pickup and stopped by the dump on the way home.

Events like these are considered memorable moments in an entry plan. Most citizens and staff members are not awaiting a major academic address or the unveiling of a complex strategic plan. They are waiting to find out if the new superintendent or principal is human and if he or she is likely to "fit in." Any entry plan ought to include taking advantage of those opportunities that permit the new leader to demonstrate his/her human side.

PLANNING THE ALL-STAFF MEETING

In nearly every district there is an all-staff meeting that kicks off the school year. For building principals, there is also a similar event on a local scale. Planning for this event should not be left to chance; rather, it should be used as the way to set the tone for the year.

The district-wide event ought to be remembered best for the fact it was surprisingly short and consisted mostly of morale boosters. The day before school starts is possibly the worst time to expect staff members to concentrate on professional development activities. They are preoccupied with the imminent arrival of their students. Their second greatest interest is being able to see people they might not have seen for several months.

With that in mind, it is a good idea to start with an informal reception that includes sweet rolls, some fruit, perhaps bagels, juice, and coffee. Planners should get someone outside of the school staff to serve it. The cooks don't want to be stuck in the kitchen while everyone else is visiting—they are part of the staff too and on this occasion ought to be relieved of their regular duties. This event will take about thirty to forty-five minutes. Some districts like to have some lively music playing in the background.

Everyone can then adjourn to a nearby gymnasium or auditorium for a brief program. The school board will likely be present for introductions. This may be the only time some staff members see them unless the community is very small. The board president might well want to bring greetings as will the new superintendent. Some districts have the cheerleaders and band present to play the fight song. Various quick elements can be added to spice up the event.

In one district, the board and administrators, who were seated in front, did a card trick which spelled out "Welcome Back." The fact that the high school principal had his "m" upside down merely added to the event. The superintendent or master of ceremonies can then remind them that everyone appreciates the fact they are under the gun and need to get to their buildings and that they will be sent on their way as quickly as possible.

Even if the setting includes spending a larger share of the day in smaller group or departmental meetings, it is important to make sure the time formally gathered in neat rows is mixed up with time to move around and share ideas.

New building principals will want to follow much the same pattern and provide ample time for work in classrooms. The agenda for the building-level meeting ought to be just as upbeat and include only the basics in terms of items for discussion or presentation. This is not the time for the staff to collectively develop goals for the coming year or hear a lengthy presentation about the new reading program. They want to get to their rooms and get ready for the students—even if some of them have been there since the first day of August setting up.

It is best to build a calendar that provides in-service time during the year when staff are better able to focus rather than stacking up those days at the beginning of school.

BEING HELPFUL

Depending upon the size of the district, the role of the new superintendent during the early days of school can vary. For the most part, the superintendent will want to help facilitate a smooth opening. Most new administrators have a month or two in advance of opening day to get their feet on the ground and handle their own duties and demands. By the time the staff gets there, they should be in a position to focus their time and energy entirely on assisting staff. Even in larger districts, superintendents have been known to help with lunchroom duty, pass out materials, greet parents and students, or perform a variety of other functions which both provide visibility and provide a helpful service at the same time.

It is important to make sure staff members are doing the same. In many districts, on the first day, students and parents are held at bay until a magic hour. Other districts have chosen more of an open house format, encouraging parents to come to the classrooms with their student and perhaps enjoy a cookie or a cup of coffee. It sets a much more positive tone.

Chapter 3

RELATIONSHIPS

There will come a time when the new principal or superintendent will actually be able to begin framing strategic educational initiatives designed to move the academic program forward, improve student achievement, address building needs, and shape the budgeting process. However, this probably won't occur anytime within the first six months in office—at least not successfully. It may not occur within the first year.

> *A realtor suggested that when buying a house, rather than redoing the yard the first month of occupancy, it's not a bad idea to wait and see what comes up in the spring. That's not a bad concept for school administrator to consider when taking on a new job.*

The first six months need to be primarily devoted to the development of relationships and trust. Good salesmen know that they first need to focus on the needs of the customer and establish rapport before they move forward with their marketing efforts.

Boards may well give new administrators marching orders in terms of some of things they wish to have accomplished. But the assessments of performance by new administrators—particularly at the outset—will be based upon the development of their relationships with staff, students, and the community.

The telephones of board members do not ring off the hook with complaints about whether or not new materials are being reviewed or whether or not the new principal has meticulously charted student test scores and is carefully planning a series of interventions in specific areas where the children are weak. They ring off the hook if the new principal is unfair and inconsistent with discipline, rarely attends football games, skips PTSA meetings, is coming down hard on long-time staff members, or has joined the Lions Club but never attends.

DEFINING A PLACE IN THE COMMUNITY

A new superintendent or principal has the luxury of enjoying immediate prestige and social status in a community that is not generally accorded to other new arrivals. This is based upon acceptance of the fact that while small communities are places where acceptance is marked by generations of residence, the school administration is generally exempted because of their transitory nature.

In addition, due to the fact that in small communities the school is generally a major employer, the leader of that organization has instant influence. Even knowing this, it is important for the new administrator not to become enamored with this fact or isolated. Added advice would include a reminder communications and conversations should be designed to inform, not to impress.

Good administrators work for all parents and need to make efforts to find ways to touch base with a broad range of their constituency—not just the Rotarians, Kiwanians, or the Chamber.

DEVELOPING A REALISTIC BALANCE

> *"New administrators have an innate desire to be all things to all people. In so doing, they create an impossible work schedule and become immersed in petty details and uses of their valuable time and training which are by no means cost-effective. In picking up loose ends which include bus duty, lunch duty, and a host of similar assignments, administrators are engaged in performing duties that could be handled by staff members making far less per hour. It is vital for new administrators to quickly develop strategies for dispensing with the trivia in exchange for finding the time and energy to address the real leadership needs of the assignment. Most often those needs are closely aligned with instruction or the improvement of student achievement."*

There are studies that suggest that almost half of those entering the teaching profession leave within the first five years. Often it's due to lack of support. Quite probably, there are also many new small school administrators who struggle during those early years because a support system is not in place.

One of the keys to survival is the development of some type of support system—not a crutch, but a realistic system that provides time for reflection on the job and open, nonthreatening opportunities to contemplate the job. In some cases, there are mentoring programs in place that provide that support. In other districts, particularly those with only one or two administrators, it might be necessary to look elsewhere for such a structure. In some programs, the approach to mentoring is called coaching. Whatever the name, such a program provides the opportunity for reflective conversations, emotional and moral support, and affirmations regarding job performance.

Chapter Four

Effective Leadership and Decision-Making Practices

EFFECTIVE LEADERSHIP PRACTICES

There are many terms that describe effective leadership practices. Some of the most relevant descriptions are those which have been extracted from administrative searches. These include such practices as delegation, a service orientation, openness, democracy, organization, ethics, the use of humor, and a capacity for multi-tasking.

They also suggest that administrators need to develop a clear understanding of the role they are about to assume. The list below provides some examples of those qualities identified by district search teams:

- "Is comfortable delegating authority to other administrators and supervisory personnel"
- "A belief that leadership is a service occupation"
- "An open, visible, and accessible leadership style with the ability to foster open dialogue and mutual respect"
- "The ability to provide effective team leadership for a strong management team and staff while using a participatory leadership style"
- "Experience administering a small school district"
- "Has demonstrated management and organizational skills which allow for effective leadership through delegation and accountability"
- "Team leadership skills that demonstrate ethical behavior, integrity, and a sense of humor"

- "An understanding and appreciation of the multiple roles required of a superintendent in a small district, and demonstrated expertise of the skills required for success in this position."

THE SOCCER COACH

A friend had a son who decided to turn out for soccer. Several years later, the father was recruited to be the assistant coach although he knew little, if anything, about the game. The head coach indicated that with fourteen young men in his charge, he basically needed someone to assist with crowd control. Little did he know at the time that two weeks later his construction firm would get a major contract out-of-town and the new assistant was about to experience a promotion.

This new experience as the head coach became part of several important lessons he learned from the game of soccer.

The first lesson actually began several years earlier. When his son first became involved, the team consisted of five and six-year-olds. Wherever the ball was, there they were—chasing it en masse. While they had rudimentary position assignments, that had little to do with where they were on the field. Wherever the ball was, there was the entire team.

As he watched his son's soccer team evolve over the next few years and as the team members grew from five and six-year-olds to nine and ten-year-olds. The transformation was amazing. Not only did they gain in skills and coordination, they also developed an appreciation for the importance of playing their assigned positions rather than having everyone chase the same ball all over the field.

Many times since, in looking at the organization of much larger and sophisticated entities, it is easy to reflect back on those same fundamental concepts—rather than having everyone chase the same ball, it makes more sense for each member of the management team to play their positions.

Prior to his elevation to the head job, the contributions of the assistant had consisted largely of crowd control and serving as the second driver, since the team needed to divide the fourteen players between two vehicles. He also had developed a remote familiarity with the modest equipment inventory. Being head coach also meant becoming immersed in the strategy of the game.

Fortunately, this was a team of young men ten and under so there wasn't an expectation they would be scouting opponents, spending Sunday afternoons examining game films, creating scouting teams, and developing elaborate game plans. The team practiced two afternoons a week and played games on Tuesdays and Saturdays.

Fortuitously, the mother of one of the team members was British and married to a doctor from New Zealand. She was a valuable source of insight into the intricacies of the game since she and her husband had both grown up in countries where soccer was a historical part of the culture. What strategy the new head coach employed in terms of preparation came from the doctor's wife.

For his part, the coach had the good sense not to try telling the team members what he did not know. It was interesting how the team evolved. Prior to the moment the head coach departed, the team had lost more games than it had won. The original coach, who was a student of soccer and who knew every aspect of the game, was an active participant from the sidelines as he continually provided instructions.

In retrospect, his contributions may have been more distracting and confusing to the ten-year-olds who were simultaneously trying to concentrate on the game and hear what he had to say. They spent a good bit of time looking at the coach while things they should have been paying attention to unfolded around them.

Without an extensive soccer background, all the new team leader could really do was make sure the team had a sufficient number of players on the field and yell encouragement. He certainly couldn't yell strategy or suggestions because the team members knew more about what they ought to do than he did. The new coach spent the rest of the season as their cheerleader and as the individual who provided support in terms of making sure they had what they needed to play the game and were where they needed to be.

He also tried to provide a measure of added value through helping build their confidence, their belief in their ability to win, and the knowledge that each of them was making a contribution.

On the field, the players worked their hearts out while the adults on the sidelines yelled encouragement and nothing more. Surprisingly, the team won the rest of its games and the league championship.

It was an interesting lesson in the value of empowerment for everyone involved.

A BASIS FOR DECISION MAKING

In beginning a discussion of decision making, an effective point of departure is to examine the descriptions that boards and districts have given in terms of their expectations for new administrators. Some of these would include:

- "The ability to empower others and to support them in the process. The willingness to consider all sides of an issue and the courage to then make a decision"
- "Has a heart for children and is committed to student-centered decisions"
- "Can accommodate stress and make courageous decisions"
- "A concerted focus on making decisions based on the best interests of students"
- "The ability to make tough decisions based upon research and accurate information"
- "Possesses the skills to facilitate team success and believes in a management system based upon empowerment and delegation"
- "Is a decisive and positive administrator, able to provide strong leadership in the resolution of tough problems. Has a record of making fair, consistent, and courageous decisions, even under significant pressure"
- "Is an accomplished problem-solver who can think creatively."

In looking through these, and in working with a variety of boards, patterns do begin to emerge. In fact, many of the comments included above represent different ways of saying much the same thing about delegation and courageous decision making. Certainly one of the most prevalent patterns is the idea of capitalizing on the strengths and abilities of others in the decision-making process. . . or in other words, having the self-confidence to delegate decisions to others. A second pattern is the need to accept opinions from all sides.

Perhaps as important as accepting opinions from all sides is then having the willingness to actually make a decision. One board member, providing information about a candidate seeking another position, was asked about possible weaknesses. *"Well,"* the board member noted, *"this person is a bit random in that he goes through an awful lot of unnecessary dialogue and process before finally getting to a decision. Most of us are worn out and have almost ceased to care by the time we get there. We know where he is going, but we become a bit impatient waiting for it to happen."*

Another critical issue sounds almost like a clique but it deals with the importance of remembering that the schools are about students. Too often, boards, communities, parent groups, and administrators become bogged down in petty politics and self-interest while forgetting the central focus of the decision-making process in schools—the students.

CULTURAL CONSIDERATIONS IN DECISION MAKING

It doesn't take years of experience in small communities to realize that they are, for the most part, conservative areas that look at issues differently than people living in metropolitan communities. After all, these are places where the average annual family income in some counties might be as little $14,000 plus.

Armed with the charge of respecting "hard-earned tax dollars" and assuming that the community will appreciate any effort to cut costs, well-meaning administrators have moved forward to make ends meet without considering some of unique aspects of the job market in small towns.

For example, a $15,000-a-year classroom assistant position with precious benefits included may be one of the area's premier employment opportunities. In a metropolitan area, such a position is at the bottom of the food chain. In many rural areas, particularly the agricultural or forestry-based communities, such jobs represent family survival. And it may not be the pay, but rather the benefits, that make the difference.

> *In a Headstart classroom in Baker County operated by Eastern Oregon University (EOU) one of the site administrators noted that the aide jobs are coveted in that community because EOU pays benefits. With the rising costs of medical insurance, these aides valued the benefits more than the pay itself.*

Most teachers working in the community are relative "interlopers" in comparison with those who have claimed the coveted classified or non licensed jobs. And, generally, despite depleted enrollments and declining resources as well as a host of other rational fiscal arguments, in many cases the job as a source of employment is everything.

In one situation a district had to make the difficult choice of eliminating one of its two bus routes because there were no longer enough children to justify two. This meant eliminating the job of a long-time citizen.

The decision was of such magnitude the superintendent/principal eventually became the victim of local politics surrounding the loss of this job as a part of the community's economic base. The former bus driver ran for the school board, was elected president, and engineered the dismissal of the superintendent.

In another community, a financially-strapped district was heavily subsidizing the food service program at a time when contracting out represented tremendous savings. Concern over the loss of jobs for two long-time residents of the district eventually prevailed in the face of all other forces and facts.

In short, prospective principals and superintendents would be well-advised to remember the fragile tie between the value of school jobs in struggling rural economies and realistic and practical budget decisions—most notably with an eye toward the fact that the tie is emotional for the most part rather than rational.

In searches involving small districts consultants spend a great deal of time talking about thinking outside the box and providing new solutions, particularly when it comes to funding. Within that context, it is important not to overlook Homecoming, traditional athletic alliances, and assuring that in some ways schools look fundamentally the same as they did when the parents and other community members were in attendance.

While not all small communities are the same, there are many similarities. Most notable is the desire to retain some sense of the identity. In far too many cases, it is already too late to mirror the economic characteristics that once existed. Even the downtown business core is likely to bear little, if any resemblance to what it might have looked like a half-century or a century ago.

This leaves only the school as the last bastion of identity. The loss of the school has come to symbolize the death knell for most smaller towns and therefore the battle to retain that final vestige of community life is fought with energy and vigor.

And there are some who believe that as the last, organized industry in many small communities, the schools will somehow take on a new role as an incubator for new economic growth since they offer the only possible base for such endeavors.

MAKING THE TOUGH DECISIONS

Boards and communities have taken a variety of approaches to describing the potential new administrator in the decision-making arena. Some examples would include:

- "the ability to maintain composure and a sense of humor while under fire"
- "visionary with demonstrated success in uniting a staff and community"
- "a reputation for tough, solid, decision-making with the ability to hold the trust and respect of those who may not agree, and the ability to gain their support"
- "Fosters collaboration, listens to all sides, accepts give and take, and then acts decisively"
- "Is a strong leader capable of making courageous decisions."

When considering behavior under fire, a good rule is to remember that once the conflict has passed, it will be important to rebuild or retain relationships and that's where the focus ought to be so that bridges aren't burned in the process. Whenever possible, keep the focus on the issues, not the people involved.

In larger districts, if one administrator doesn't get along with a particular parent or constituency, it is possible that another one will. In very small communities, an administrator doesn't have that luxury since they might well be the only one in the district. If decisions are rooted in fairness and consistency and if the administrator can maintain a sense of humor and cordial relationships, most crises will ultimately pass.

As noted in the examples of criteria, districts and buildings are often seeking an administrator with the courage to ultimately make a decision. Veteran administrators often find that if they develop a pattern of seeking input, considering all sides, and then making a decision, those they are serving will develop confidence in their leadership.

On one occasion, when a decision made by an administrator ultimately proved to be unwise, he asked a long-time local parent and activist who had been involved why he hadn't raised a stink. His response was "it looks like you make pretty good decisions about ninety percent of the time. You're allowed a margin of error and this one clearly fits in the ten percent category."

> Any principal who has been involved in the oversight of the annual Holiday Program knows that the sixth graders are often reluctant participants in the grade school production. One democratic building principal decided to give them their way and let them become part of the audience. On the day of the event, hundreds of parents came to the gymnasium, many of them unaware their child would not be taking part. Within hours, if not minutes, the principal was overwhelmed by visits and calls from angry sixth-grade parents demanding an explanation. The following afternoon, the sixth-grade parents were invited to a meeting in the library. Many of them were still visibly angry when they arrived.
> The principal got up before them and said, "ever since I have been the principal, the sixth graders have said they were too old for the Holiday Program and wanted to be left out. So, I left them out. It was obviously a stupid decision on my part and one that has had a negative effect on your holiday celebrations. I can assure you that as long as I am principal of this school, the sixth graders will be very much involved in the Holiday program."
> Before she could go any further, one parent stood up and said, "you don't have to go on beating yourself up over this, anyone can make a mistake." The principal didn't make excuses, didn't attempt to whitewash the situation, and readily admitted an error and the willingness to move on. The anger and distress of the parents overwhelmingly turned into concern for the principal and her well-being.

As noted elsewhere, one board seeking a new superintendent/principal specifically looked for someone who was not afraid to admit a mistake and move on.

THE ROLE OF PERSONAL VALUES IN SCHOOL ADMINISTRATION

There are few callings more demanding in terms of personal values than school administration. Parents entrust their children to the care of the schools with a strong expectation they will be well-cared for and provided with a safe environment. The personal standards expected of school personnel are uncompromising. As a result, school boards and school districts are spending increasingly more time and effort examining the personal values of potential administrators. They are also becoming much more clear in outlining their expectations.

A perusal of recent postings for superintendents and principals illuminates the kinds of issues which boards are considering in their search for new leadership. Some of these include:

- "Reflects fundamental values such as integrity, ethical behavior, honesty, and fairness"
- "Has a record of good personal introspection in terms of taking responsibility, admitting mistakes and weaknesses, and can move forward without excuses"
- "Is forthright and willing to admit mistakes"
- "Open and collaborative leadership style with a high degree of personal ethics"
- "A record of high-level leadership performance, exhibiting diligent work habits and self-motivation"
- "Demonstration of such characteristics as integrity, honesty, ethical behavior, energy, enthusiasm, and fairness"
- "A proven record of trust, credibility, and integrity"
- "Is characterized by a high energy level, enthusiasm, and the capacity to inspire others"
- "Demonstrates a strong commitment to accountability—in oneself and others"
- "Has high standards for self and high expectations for others, holding both self and others accountable."

As can be seen, the expectations include both personal values and personal characteristics. It is interesting to note that in the case of two districts, there was concern about the willingness of administrators to admit responsibility for their errors and then demonstrate the capacity to move on. Since the criteria for administrative searches is often built on past performance of other administrators, this has obviously been an issue in some districts. This is also manifested in several comments about the importance of being personally accountable before expecting this characteristic in others.

In the course of considering coping skills through a series of tips and ideas regarding the art of surviving as a school administrator, none of the suggestions are meant to encourage an administrator to compromise his or her moral compass or personal principles in order to gain social or professional acceptance.

TIME MANAGEMENT

Some of the many studies that have talked about the incredible expectations for new superintendents and principals in rural districts have also talked about the necessity of developing schemes for time management and also the self-confidence necessary to determine priorities in the use of time.

Repeated studies have shown the critical importance of having the principal, the superintendent, and the superintendent/principal focus on instructional issues rather than being detoured into spending time on matters which, although they seem important to the constituency, detract from the primary mission of the enterprise.

It takes strong and outspoken support from the board to help the administrator be able to focus on those issues which the board feels are most important—and that usually is strongly tied to the academic success of the district's students.

Within this concept is the issue of the administrator as a manager versus the administrator as leader. The management functions are those mundane issues that consume considerable time but are rarely worth the value of the administrator in terms of effective return on performance versus compensation.

Leadership, on the other hand, is generally associated with the ability of the administrator to out-distance the value versus compensation equation.

Chapter Five

Board-Superintendent Relations

Research projects studying the factors that cause superintendents to find satisfaction in their current jobs and the factors they consider in contemplating other professional opportunities consistently center more on board-superintendent relations than on compensation and related benefits. Certainly in visiting with candidates as part of the executive search process, one of the first questions is always "tell me about the board."

There is no question that a direct correlation exists between the nature of the board and the capacity of a district to attract and retain quality leadership.

There are also varying statistics about the average tenure of superintendents but the numbers most commonly used range somewhere between 2.3 and 2.8 years. Those districts, which exceed the average range are those that have made an effort to create a professional working environment in which stability and tenure become the norm.

In the private sector, successful businesses go out of their way to attract and retain a high quality workforce. In most areas of the economy, the better the talent, the more successful the enterprise. This is certainly a critical factor in the upper echelons of leadership.

For this reason, it makes sense for school districts to carefully examine the topic of board-superintendent relations and to take the time to visit the subject regularly in order to assure that a positive relationship is being perpetuated.

As a part of most executive searches, there is a process through which the district gives careful consideration to the qualities and qualifications it seeks in a new leader. There is also an identification of the challenges, demands, and expectations for the new superintendent.

Many times, the staff, the parents, the community, and the students are engaged in the process of helping identify these issues. Unfortunately, once the superintendent is employed, there is never a discussion of the material, which was used in making the selection.

> *School boards or superintendents—depending upon whether it is a new superintendent or principal, ought to consider holding a follow-up session with their new hire within the first sixty days of employment. The purpose would be to revisit the criteria for selection, remind the new individual why they were hired, and establish two or three major expectations for the coming year. Sometimes the search consultant can be reengaged to assist with facilitation of this session*

OPERATING LIKE A BUSINESS

It has been suggested many times that schools ought to operate more like a business.

That's a tall challenge for an organization that doesn't operate with the same latitude as most private entities. And yet there are certainly many lessons that can be learned from the private sector. Some of the most obvious, of course, can be found in the arena of cost containment, customer service, responses to competition, and client satisfaction.

These latter issues are relatively new to public education and most other governmental agencies. School boards have found themselves challenged with making sure the district is functional and a positive place for students because a new factor has been introduced—the traditional public schools may not be the only game in town. Charter Schools, on-line schools, alternative schools, private schools, and other options are increasingly more accessible.

There is also a growing conversation about vouchers and choice. And, mobility isn't what it used to be. At one time, conventional wisdom suggested schools ought to be located no more than three miles apart which was the distance an average student could walk in an hour. Now most students can drive fifty to sixty miles in an hour and in some cases parents are willing to drive them.

While the rhetoric about operating more like a business comes easily, there are certainly some unique characteristics of public schools that need to be taken into consideration.

> *Jamie Vollmer is one of the founders of a prominent midwest ice cream firm who used to be a strong critic of public education. Vollmer has become a nationally prominent presenter on the challenges facing educators. At one*

time, he was so outspoken regarding the ills of public education that he was often invited to speak to groups that were likely to have a special appreciation for such philosophies.

However, he was also invited to speak to education groups as well, in part to initiate debate. One day he was holding forth in front of a group of teachers regarding the inadequacies of public education when a lady who had spent twenty-five years in the classroom stood up and began thoughtfully asking questions about the ice cream business.

"What makes your ice cream so special?" she asked. "Oh," he replied enthusiastically, "we use only the finest ingredients. They are always triple A rated, whether it is the dairy products or the ingredients. We won't settle for anything less."

"So," she said, "if you get a load of blueberries and they aren't perfect, what do you do?" "Well," he replied without hesitation, "we reject them."

"We can't do that," she said, "we have to take all of the blueberries."

This is a wonderful example of some of the fundamental differences between public education and private business. Banks don't make loans to everyone who walks through the door, although in recent years, they tried very hard to do so. The economy of an entire nation and perhaps even the world suffered as a result and they have since abandoned the practice.

A manufacturing plant doesn't necessarily accept every single part that comes its way. Businesses have the latitude of making decisions regarding what they will or won't do. Schools are much more limited in that regard. They certainly don't have the luxury of arbitrarily deciding who they will and won't serve.

Between 2007 and 2009, the author spent two-and-a-half years in the private sector as editor and publisher of a daily newspaper. If it was discovered on any given day revenues and expenditures were out of line, a plan could be in place by noon that would remedy the situation, whether it was someone's job or a service the newspaper had been offering.

A superintendent or principal who happens to be in a similar situation doesn't have the luxury of arbitrarily eliminating the band program one day or most other programs offered in the schools. Everything in education has a constituency and there isn't the same expectation schools can suddenly make the same kind of decisions that occur in the private sector.

Still, there are circumstances in which operating with sound business practices or principles does make sense. The earlier notations about compatibility between management and the board offers a good place to start. Businesses exist to create a profit and one of the very first things successful private entities do is to make sure the corporate board and the chief executive officer are on the same page working together to make that happen.

> *There are some who think it is important for the board and superintendent to be on opposite sides of the table in order to assure accountability. This is sometimes predicated by the notion that boards don't want to appear to "rubber stamp" the proposals from the superintendent. When good board-superintendent relations exist, the professional leader is not likely to advance proposals or solutions, which are incompatible with the ideals expressed by the board. Therefore, it won't be surprising if everyone generally appears to be on the same page most of the time.*

Likewise, stability contributes in a positive way to the achievement of long-term goals. Rapid turnover does not produce stability, the achievement of goals, consistent fiscal management and oversight, or ongoing program development. Nor is rapid turnover in the top leadership ranks a viable element of accountability.

Recently, a district that is "hard on its superintendents" and creates rapid turnover suddenly discovered that its cash balance had gone from $720,000 to $18,000 in two years—all of which was a giant surprise. Too much turnover means starting over...again, and again, and again.

The profit motive isn't unique to business. In the case of a school district, it is important to make sure that every single child profits from his or her educational experience. The children served by the district count on the adults to practice and model effective, positive, and productive leadership.

Every successful business has a plan. Once the business plan is adopted, they stick to that plan. It can be revisited periodically, but otherwise it is important to stay the course. With limited resources, it is particularly critical that a district carefully and sensitively adopt its priorities through some meaningful process. Otherwise, it will be like traveling without a roadmap—they are liable to end up anywhere.

All involved with education in a particular district look to the board for guidance. If the board is going in all sorts of directions, it shouldn't be surprising that everyone else is as well. Here is a basic question to ask in terms of planning: Does the district or building have goals? If not, are they planning to set them? It helps to have goals so that people can't continually derail the spending plan and the focus of district energies. In an age of limited resources, it is particularly critical to have a sophisticated expenditure plan which matches the direction and mission of the district.

One of the most defining attributes of a successful business is the environment in which people function and hundreds of books are being written on the subject. There is a growing focus on climate in the workplace and worker satisfaction.

For what might be the first time in history, individuals from four different generations are now in the workplace together. Administrators in all situations would be wise to gain an understanding of generational differences and how those differences impact work styles and worker expectations.

Within the school setting, it is clear students learn best in a positive environment. School employees work longer and harder when they feel good about what they are doing. Parents need to have confidence in their child's school.

The community wants to be proud of its schools. New businesses won't locate in towns where the schools are in an uproar. In some small communities, the aura around the schools is incredibly positive and the schools are thriving. In others, it is almost completely dysfunctional. Once the dysfunctional symptoms start, it becomes like an infection and everyone ultimately loses.

Being involved in dozens of superintendent searches, means going into many districts and having an opportunity to get a firsthand look at how things are going. Sometimes, of course, the district is replacing a retiree or someone who has received a promotion, but since the mission is always to find new leadership, there is a better than average chance of encountering a dysfunctional situation.

Most often, that situation can be traced right to the top--the board and superintendent. There is always a fine line between a smooth operation and a dysfunctional unit. In many ways, it is like a successful athletic team. When members play their position, the team wins. When individuals overlook their roles and put teamwork on the back burner, winning is much less likely.

Going back to the athletic example, sometimes in the heat of a game, individual players will try to take things into to their own hands with nothing but good intentions. They step out of the game plan for what seems to them to be all of the right reasons. The same thing happens with board members who want to be helpful to constituents by taking matters into their own hands. Or with board members who come to the table with pre-determined agendas. This isn't an individual endeavor; it requires a majority vote of the board to take action. An individual board member has no statutory authority to act independently (with the exception, to some degree, of the board president).

Perhaps one of the most misused terms in education today is that of micromanagement. Very often when beginning the process of finding new leadership, the term micromanagement comes to the surface. There is no question that even in the best of situations, some board members simply cannot avoid the temptation to step from the policy role into management.

But for every situation of inappropriate assumption of authority called micromanagement, there are an equal number of situations in which the practice is the product of default.

> *When there is no confidence in the ability of the administrator or when the administrator becomes indecisive, unresponsive, or relegates basic decisions to the board rather than assuming responsibility, micromanagement becomes a natural outgrowth. Strong, confident leaders willing to make the hard decisions are less likely to experience this phenomenon.*

In communities where the economy is struggling, it is particularly important to make sure that the schools are a place of order, predictability, sensitivity, and hope. The homes of children in a struggling community often reflect much the opposite. School is their anchor.

A local district recently asked for a superintendent search in a situation where two members had just been declared ineligible to serve because of the fact that they were elected to office but did not reside in their director districts. A recall effort was aimed at three more because of concerns for the two who were dropped from the district and disagreements over staffing levels and funding support levels for the various areas of the county.

The district was being torn apart by this feud and much of the energy was being directed at the controversy—not toward the kids. Since this happened in the midst of the search, the district was unable to put its best foot forward.

Good things happen when the major players respect each other…their opinions, their interests, their skills, their needs, and their respective roles and potential contributions. It serves the interests of the children when the adults involved in the equation feel morally and ethically obligated to model the best way to conduct business.

It isn't necessary for the board to "rubber stamp" all decisions or to agree on every issue—only that they operate with goodwill, civility, and good faith and accept and support a group decision once it has been made. And, in the process, they respect a divergence of opinions and ideas.

One of the biggest challenges of quality governance is learning to be engaged in meaningful debate or consideration of an issue and then demonstrating the willingness to accept and support the decision of the majority. Most experienced board members have found themselves in both the majority and the minority at different times.

As part of the equation, board members need to stand for the importance of employing found fiscal practices and operating in the sunlight. One rule of thumb is the idea that if something can't be readily understood by the readers of the local newspaper in one paragraph then perhaps it ought not be done. Those involved in the management of a school district should be able to sleep well each night knowing they have nothing to fear or hide. They may not always do the right thing, but if their motives are pure and they are trying to do the right thing, that's the best anyone can hope for.

Business publications often list things like the "100 best companies to work for." Such ratings are becoming more and more important as competition for skilled workers grows.

Potential employees often review such ratings before choosing where they want to work. School districts are no different. If a district has a reputation for rapid turnover and extensive in-fighting, the best teachers will look elsewhere for jobs.

And, despite all the advancements that have been made in technology, the interaction between the teacher and the student still remains at the heart of the education equation. Knowing that makes it clear why districts need to be able to hire and retain the best teachers possible.

The school district mentioned earlier—the one with a feuding board of education—probably had more openings in August than it did in May or June. Teachers are jumping ship whenever they can to take jobs in other nearby districts where there isn't so much negativity and disharmony. Teachers ask themselves, "why work in an embarrassing situation with all the fighting when they can go next-door and work where it's not only peaceful, but fun as well?"

There is always a shortage of top-tier teachers and districts that are genuinely committed to hiring the best know full well their reputation is a critical part of the recruitment equation.

As noted earlier, the board legally functions only as a team. As individuals, board members are basically interested private citizens, albeit more interested than most. Board members may receive information, but should avoid making action promises such as, "I will take care of that." Rather, the appropriate response is "thank you for the information, I will refer it to the right person in the district who can look into it" or simply suggest that the individual contact the right person directly.

Nothing undermines the effectiveness of district staff any faster than having Board members—as individuals—in the schools or out in the community making public judgments, providing direction, or making promises. Even worse, perhaps, is a grandstand effort for the benefit of patrons, which disregards the integrity, worth, and contributions of staff members.

Boards have dual roles—their governance function and that of an employer and as employers, boards are responsible for making sure they treat their employees as they, themselves, would wish to be treated—fairly, honestly, and with dignity.

Communication is one of the most critical roles of both the superintendent and the board. While it is important to employ well-qualified leaders, their mission, as has been noted several times, in terms of communicating with the public is to inform…not impress. It is never a good practice to talk down to community members or employees.

Most boards initially worry the superintendent won't stay long enough. The average tenure is historically short, however if boards genuinely continued to worry about the superintendent leaving and transformed that into creating an environment designed to make departure a difficult decision, most superintendents would stay longer. Statistics show that a good working relationship, support, encouragement, and appreciation are the most important factors to employees.

> During a crisis in a small district involving a parent and a coach the board didn't appear to provide as much support as the superintendent wanted. One member noted superintendents come and go while the other residents of the community have to live together for years, if not generations. If that's the case, boards should not be surprised if they are experiencing somewhat rapid turnover even if the individual they hired is someone they want very much to keep.

GETTING AN EFFECTIVE WORKING RELATIONSHIP STARTED AND SETTING THE GROUND RULES

During the hiring process, considerable attention is often given to identifying qualifications and qualities of the candidates and the challenges facing a new principal or superintendent. However, once that process has been completed, it is, as has been discussed, seldom revisited. Boards and superintendents need to consider where the district is and where it needs to go.

> *"The hardest thing about genuinely moving forward is letting go of the past."*

A good place to start is to have the board conduct a review of past practices and frustrations. While they don't want to dredge up a whole load of past problems, it is vital that the fundamental differences and sources of concern be laid openly on the table in the district.

There are always some tough issues in that regard, but they need to at least acknowledge what happened in order to help avoid having them happen again. In the case of a building principal, the superintendent can outline some of his/her concerns about how the building has been operated in the past.

This is a productive use of past history. For the most part, however, as a matter of common practice, there is no point in looking back unless there is an intention to go there.

New administrators will want to ask questions such as: How do board members see their role—what are their major roles as members of the board? What are appropriate actions and concerns and what might be construed as micromanagement? The primary roles of the board include:

- oversight of the district's financial affairs;
- approval of personnel actions; and
- guidance in providing balanced program development.

A second question would be: How does the superintendent see the board's role—what is the superintendent looking for from the board? What are the critical elements in working successfully together as a team?

The board/executive relationship is not the typical employer/employee relationship, but rather a team relationship. The board hires the executive and delegates all management responsibility to that person. It is the board's job to monitor the executive's work, but not to interfere with daily management. The executive, on the other hand, is a member of the board team and should be expected to be advisor, consultant, and partner to the board on all matters. The expectation of support for decisions should go both ways.

> One veteran administrator tells about the night he was making a presentation to the board and was asking for a specific decision. Much to his surprise, the board did not agree with his assessment of the situation.
> As he was leaving the meeting, visibly frustrated over that fact, a twenty-four-year veteran said "you're not very happy with our decision, are you." "No," he admitted, "I'm not."
> "Well, young man," she said, "what makes you think the board is in love with all the decision you make?"

It does cut both ways.

While the board delegates all management, it does not give up absolute responsibility for all that happens in the organization. The executive has a strong obligation to report to the board about the management of the organization. Board supervision of the executive should be by the full board and not by individual members.

Several local boards have begun asking two important questions at their annual retreat that help contribute to the ongoing development of a stronger, more open working relationship:

- Are there areas where the board could be more helpful to the superintendent?
- Are there areas where the superintendent could be more helpful to the board?

In the case of principals, what will be the relationship between the principal and the superintendent? How will they communicate? What does the superintendent need to know? How much decision-making power does the superintendent wish to retain? Does the superintendent wish to have principals interacting with board members?

In practice, the board really has only one employee, the superintendent. Employees need to clearly understand who gives the orders, who is accountable to whom, and who has responsibility for what. It is important for the board to create operating principles which they have in place including a chain of command that sets up clear lines of authority and accountability. Some boards have these guidelines embedded in policy.

Another important question might be: Does the superintendent or principal's vision for the job coincide with the board's or (in the case of a principal) with the superintendent's?

At the outset, it is imperative to develop a set of operating principles including topics such as:

- How the board will handle telephone calls/being cornered by constituents.
- Agreeing on a procedure for open communication between the board and the administrative team.
- Creating a process for getting emergency information to the board.
- Having a process for getting regular information to the board (making sure everyone is part of the loop). Carefully cultivate a working environment which does not exclude anyone from equal communication.
- Agreeing to disagree and supporting the outcome.
- Developing board agendas.
- Promoting on-going board training—making it a commitment to be proud of and not apologizing for attending training that improves performance – "we want strong staff development for everyone in the district and that begins with our board".
- Avoiding springing surprises on one another.
- Making sure the superintendent provides adequate backup material surrounding important decisions—and taking the time to ask questions in advance.
- Helping the board president with well-established meeting procedures.
- Only making decisions as a board and then having the courage to support the decision once it has been made.
- Referring complaints to the superintendent—asking the superintendent to provide a response regarding how it was handled.
- Having established procedures for dealing with the media.
- Discussing the role of the board as a visible part of the district team…at events, visiting programs, etc.
- Remembering that the primary identity of the board is with the community…not with the staff. Sometimes boards can become torn and forget who elected them and who they represent.
- Promoting civilized disagreement.

For a superintendent or a principal going into a new position, it is important to revisit the hiring process and to ask key questions based upon the reason why he or she was hired:

- Why the choice—what strengths did they see?
- How do these strengths relate to the needs of the district?
- What are the primary performance expectations?
- In June of next year, in what ways should the building or district be different?
- What are two or three major issues that need attention during the coming year?

Added Note: Have the board focus on the ends to be accomplished and avoid the temptation to prescribe the means. Also, have them make sure to identify the things that won't be tolerated—the hot buttons, the chuckholes, board standards, and the sacred cows. For both superintendents and principals, it is important to know and understand the rules...particularly those that aren't in the district's policy manual.

A veteran board secretary can be an invaluable source of guidance regarding things to avoid or be aware of when dealing with the board.

CAPITALIZING ON BOARD INTERESTS OR STRENGTHS

Sometime micromanagement is confused with specific areas of focus or interest by board members. Astute administrators can sometimes turn those areas of focus and interest into a positive.

In one district, there was a board member who spent hours poring over the monthly bill report. After spending a morning on the process, he used to drop by the office and ask two or three questions about various bills. The superintendent would then find him the answers and report back. That portion of the process generally took less than fifteen minutes. Eventually, the superintendent ceased devoting so much time to reviewing the bill summary knowing full well that this conscientious board member would do it for him.

The board member was retired, was interested, was intent on providing a high level of scrutiny, and was very serious about the task. The superintendent capitalized on his interest and it became a real time-saver.

Another board member was a construction expert and was willing to spend an extensive amount of time reviewing the building projects. It was suggested that the board create a building committee that included a board member who could then represent the interests of the board and the superintendent in the process. He was careful not to step over the line with the district's project manager and was primarily valuable in a consultant-type role. Since he was a board member, not a lot of time was spent at board meetings discussing building projects. For the most part, they trusted his judgment and respected his experience.

There are board members who enjoy, or at least are willing, to spend countless hours reading RFPs, contracts, and similar documents. They are quite likely going to do it whether the superintendent likes it or not so in that vein, the administrator might just as well find a way to make it a positive contribution to the operation rather than a negative intrusion.

Along the way there have been banking committees, auditing committees, curriculum committees, superintendent selection committees, and negotiating committees to involve and capitalize on the expertise and interests of board members. It takes the edge from micromanagement and channels energies and interests in a productive way.

FACTORS THAT DISCOURAGE ADMINISTRATORS

One of the major factors, that frustrates or discourages administrators includes compensation. Ironically, even though compensation may cause teachers to decide administration isn't worth it, the lack of pay in relation to time demands and responsibility rarely causes practicing administrators to leave the field.

Some of the other factors that cause job frustration include job stress, excessive time requirements, the difficulties of meeting parental and staff demands, and social demands within the school, which prevent a focus on the major issues. Some other issues might include job complexity and workload, national, state, and district pressures, political stresses, and lack of authority to actually effect change.

These are listed not because they are performance targets but because they identify the potential considerations that might cause administrators to flee the job. If they know in advance what the major challenges might be, they are better prepared to take deliberate action to reduce the likelihood they will become roadblocks to successful performance.

Chapter Six

Developing An Effective Format For Board Meetings, *Or* "Nothing Good Happens After 8 p.m."

"It is important to remember that the law requires the board to meet in public, not necessarily with the public."

GENERAL FORMAT

The most effective guideline in creating a framework for board meetings is to establish a format the district can live with in good times and bad—or in other words, that can accommodate the issues they want to hear and don't want to hear. The guidelines that apply to good news must be consistent when bad news comes.

Sometimes boards lapse into the habit of informal interaction with attendees—particularly when attendance only includes a couple of regulars. Such familiarity can create problems when fifty people show up to talk about a controversial issue. In most cases, it is better to use a modest level of protocol and formality on a regular basis.

THE BOARD'S PRIORITIES

The best way to determine what a board feels is important is to observe three or four board meetings and record the time allotted for various topics. What the board feels is important is what they discuss, not that which they profess to be important. This is also the message that is radiated to the community and to the staff. This same concept quite probably extends to a measurement of the time administrators devote to various parts of the educational program.

Beginning each meeting with a student presentation or report on the students serves as a reminder why the district exists. The South Umpqua School District in Southwestern Oregon starts each meeting with "And How Are The Children?"

Even something more simple like having a student lead the flag salute and a brief presentation by various classes regarding projects, trips, or other activities gets things off on a positive note. Student recognition is also a good way to provide a positive launching point for meetings.

Knowing that parents primarily care about two things—who is teaching their children and what they are teaching them, celebrating the educational process and the success of students and staff is a reminder of what the work of the board should be all about. The elected board members are essentially the educational leaders of the school district and are responsible for creating a positive learning environment in which teachers and other staff members can perform effectively and in which students can reach high levels of achievement.

Much has been said and written about accountability within the educational structure and its contribution to improved performance. Not nearly enough has been written and said about the critical relationship between a positive working and learning environment and its relationship to improved performance.

Creation of a positive environment for the children of the district begins with the board.

ROOM ARRANGEMENT

Boards should give thought to the arrangement of the room for their meetings. The ideal arrangement is when the board can organize some type of U-shaped configuration at the front of the room with the bottom end open to attendees. This way the board can see one another and dialogue effectively and the audience is also strategically located to hear. This also provides for a separation and creates a different kind of atmosphere than having people sitting along the wall in a circle around (and behind) board members.

While most board meetings in small districts are usually characterized by a sparse audience, there are occasions when larger crowds attend. Even though the meeting is among the members of the board, sometimes having a public address system in place helps to assure everyone can hear what is taking place.

In some cases, the superintendent sits on one end—not in the middle. After all, it is the board that is meeting and the president should run the meeting. A good rule of thumb for superintendent contributions during the meeting is to remember that "less is more."

STREAMLINING MEETINGS

Many boards like to use a consent agenda that includes routine activities and reports from administrators and supervisors. These written reports should be provided to board members in advance of the meeting along with materials about the meeting. Board members who have specific questions about the reports can call the appropriate party for clarification. Such a process will also streamline meetings.

In some districts, the superintendent and principals simply highlight a few of the items from their report.

WORKSHOPS OR WORK SESSIONS

By streamlining the actual business portion of the meeting, the board will then find that it has time to incorporate workshop topics. This procedure also allows for clarification between what is a workshop and what is the business at hand.

For example, at the March meeting, the board might hold a workshop from 6:00-7:00 p.m. to discuss options for renovating a school, development of the budget, ways to streamline the curriculum, ideas for cutting costs, strategies for improving student achievement, or some other topic. This is the time when individual board members can share their general thoughts about a whole range of things. Separating work sessions from business meetings is an important reminder of the two major roles at play—managing the district and establishing policies, goals, and guidelines.

Then, at 7:00 p.m., the Board can convene its regular meeting to conduct the formal business. The actual business should, for the most part, be limited to those issues that require the board's attention. This systematic approach via the workshop format gives the board time to focus on the more weighty issues that need to be addressed while at the same time limiting board agendas to appropriate topics.

> In one district, board meetings begin at 6 p.m. with a one-hour workshop whenever there is a topic that demands the need for a workshop. Some of the topics have included the development of a staffing model, defining the objec-

tives of the secondary curriculum, creation of a master contract, an affordable athletic program, identification of short-term maintenance needs and a long-range facilities plan, procedures for building the budget, and strategies for improving student achievement.

The business meeting begins at 7 p.m. with the objective of adjourning promptly at 8 p.m. Business not handled by 8 p.m. might be postponed until the next meeting. The workshop provides an effective avenue for board members to share their thoughts about the direction of the district and to provide members of the administrative staff with insight into their expectations.

During the formal business meeting, the entire focus is on the board's policy-making role. The Board is so serious about this model that they frequently reference the fact that "nothing good happens after 8 p.m." Obviously the world won't come to an end if the meeting runs longer, but in general, boards that have developed the habit of meeting until the wee hours are generally improperly immersed in the management function of district affairs.

GENERAL THOUGHTS

The workshop/formal meeting format has been tried in several districts and is proving to be popular. Many board members have thoughts and ideas they wish to share with their fellow board members and the administration but have never known for sure exactly where this ought to occur. As a result, many good ideas have simply not been shared since there is uncertainty about the appropriate time.

The whole idea of the formal meeting/work session format isn't to stifle board participation but rather to honor the fact board members bring important things to the table that often never get expressed because there is no vehicle for doing so.

This structure provides an avenue by which the district is able to capture the thoughts, expectations, and philosophies of its governing board in a systematic fashion while also handling its policy-making and business function in a professional manner.

Chapter Seven

Creating An Administrative Evaluation System

Some years ago a district superintendent was preparing the annual evaluation for a new principal. During the course of the dialogue, he shared some things he had hoped the new principal would have accomplished in her new assignment that year. "May I be frank?" she asked. She was encouraged to share her ideas which she proceeded to do. "If you had some thoughts about what you wanted me to do at Edison School this year, it would have been enormously helpful if you had told me what they were last Fall."

That honest insight laid the foundation for an orientation program for new principals that was put into the place the following year in her district. It also laid the foundation for making sure that careful attention was given to expectations and that they were clearly outlined.

This concept seems pretty basic and anything but rocket science and yet it is a practice that is rarely implemented. In the chapter entitled "Setting the Stage for Superintendent-Board Relations," reference is made to the need for new administrators and their supervisors (either the board or the superintendent depending on if it is a principal or superintendent) to sit down together at the outset and discuss a number of critical issues.

As the search and selection process itself unfolds, careful attention is given to identifying the traits desired in the new administrator. Attention is also given to the challenges which that person will face. Then the hiring takes place and further dialogue needs to occur and become part of the evaluation process.

Chapter 7
EVALUATION INSTRUMENTS

Education agencies have spent countless hours and a ton of money studying and developing evaluation instruments. Such instruments range anywhere from a blank sheet of paper to complex measurement devices. They might include a few performance criteria or detailed performance indicators.

The process can also include complex formulas, exhaustive procedures and evaluation timelines and calendars. Sometimes administrators will prepare a self-evaluation for submission to the board or evaluation input that might include anything from detailing professional activities and community service to a listing of professional growth efforts and various other accomplishments.

At the same time, individual board members might also be asked to prepare their individual responses to the evaluation document and criteria before coming together as a group to share their collective opinions.

In some cases, districts might choose to use a comprehensive input system that includes feedback from a wide variety of audiences or stakeholders. While this is certainly valuable input, the information which is gleaned might be just as pertinent for the evaluators as it is for the evaluatee since hopefully the person being evaluated is carrying out the wishes of his or her employer. Sometimes the feedback might actually be a measurement of that direction.

> *In the end, the most valuable commodities in the evaluation process are trust, good faith, and honest, open dialogue. Without those elements the most complex instruments in the world are doomed to failure.*

Since it relates somewhat to the evaluation concept, there is an example that occurred in a district several years ago involving negotiations. During an executive session of the board outlining the parameters for the response to the union proposal, board members made it very clear that the administrators were to hold the line and not give in to further demands.

A month later, at a second executive session, one of the board members said that the teachers were complaining that the administration was too rigid in the negotiations process and that it was stifling the likelihood of reaching a settlement. The board member asked if this were, in fact, true. Fortunately, another member reminded the board that the administrators were simply carrying out the directives they had received from the board in the first place.

This example does demonstrate one of the potential pitfalls of soliciting and using feedback from a wide audience in that some of the feedback may well be the result of an administrator simply carrying out the wishes of the board.

A number of districts have adopted a process which is generally called the 360-degree method, which involves soliciting input from every available source regarding the performance of the superintendent. This works if the board is willing relegate a measure of direction for the superintendent to a host of other stakeholders besides themselves since one potential pitfall is the fact a major focus of the superintendent's energy will be on making sure everyone is happy.

In instances where the board might want the superintendent to take some potentially controversial actions or resolve some festering issues, an overriding mandate regarding universal satisfaction may not contribute effectively to the equation.

Too often, the focus is on the instrument rather than the dialogue and the quality of the interaction which transpires between the administrator and the evaluator or evaluators. In many cases, board members will huddle for hours seeking to prepare a meaningful evaluation report for the administrator when they often lack the necessary depth or scope of observations to complete many of the sections.

Most board members are readily able to assess such issues as board-superintendent relations or the quality of communications with the board. They may also have direct insight into understanding of policy, budget development, and similar functions. But when it comes to interaction with staff or most other performance items that occur all day, every day within the district itself, they have little basis upon which to make the assessments because they are rarely present to observe those issues in any depth.

As a result, those measures are typically based upon isolated scraps of information and are generally skewed toward problems rather than successes, since negative information is much more likely to be reported than routine positive issues.

In typical evaluation procedures, once the board has completed its lengthy huddle, a final evaluation is prepared and the board president meets with the superintendent to share the results. This latter process generally takes a very short time. Sometimes the entire board may be present in executive session to present the evaluation, but the time spent in such a process is typically far less than that devoted to the original discussion.

Consider the value of reversing that process and seeking to develop a system in which the bulk of the time is devoted at the outset to a meeting between the board and administrator to discuss the performance issues and dialogue about each item. The administrator can provide clarification and answer questions. The board can seek additional insight on specific matters. Once that has occurred, the board is armed with additional data to use in the preparation of the final evaluation report.

Again, much of the value of the entire evaluation process is manifested in the dialogue that occurs between the administrator and the board. This is a process which is easily transferable to evaluation of a principal by the superintendent.

PUTTING INTEGRITY INTO THE PROCESS

Earlier, a point was made about the importance of sharing expectations at the outset. It is critical that boards and administrators are clear about those issues that will be measured in the evaluation process. It is equally important to be sure that the evaluation is primarily limited to those items in order to maintain the integrity of the process.

Nothing will cause the value of the process to break down quicker than having board members or superintendents produce additional issues or expectations after the fact.

Likewise, it is important to remember that wise administrators will use the material encompassed in the evaluation as a guide to their priorities and performance during the coming year. If a single board member has included some specific area of interest in the evaluation document, the rest of the board members need to either agree to delete the item as not being part of the marching orders or agree that it is an important directive. If it's there, it will probably be addressed.

For example, if a board member is heavily into working with the local community college to develop mathematics classes for broadcast as distance learning opportunities and if the evaluation reflects the fact that the superintendent and administrators need to put more effort into this area, it shouldn't come as a surprise if the district suddenly spends thousands of dollars creating classes and having staff on-line offering trigonometry, calculus, or geometry to anyone who is interested.

It doesn't work to suddenly discover the expenditures at mid-year, wonder why they are happening, and respond with "oh, you should have known the board as a whole doesn't really believe we ought to be spending money there, that's just a personal interest that David has and we just included it in your evaluation because he made such a big point of it."

Administrators need to continually work with boards to assure that the integrity of the evaluation process is maintained at all cost so that it becomes the template upon which progress becomes written.

REGULAR INPUT

Boards ought to meet at least twice a year with their chief administrator to discuss the state of affairs in the district. The board president ought to also refer any ongoing items of concern to the superintendent in a timely manner. The same process should also be in effect between principals and superintendents.

While it isn't necessarily an administrative item in exactly the same context, an example was an incident which occurred between a principal and his head custodian. When the principal prepared the annual evaluation of the custodian in May, he noted a concern about the misuse of school equipment. The custodian asked about the notation and was advised that in October of that year, the custodian had allegedly taken home a piece of school equipment and used it to clean the carpets in his home. In the end, the validity of the concern was obscured by the fact that it might have been more appropriate to have addressed the issue in October rather than saving it up for eight months for inclusion in the evaluation.

The same principles apply in communication between boards and superintendents and between superintendents and principals.

While the annual evaluation is certainly a ritual that requires special attention, a genuinely effective process is fluid and occurs best through continuous, ongoing, meaningful feedback.

Again, the rudiments of a meaningful evaluation are not so much rooted in the capacity of boards to provide insight into complex educational issues as they are in the willingness and ability of the governing body to quantify their expectations clearly and concisely and share those expectations with the individuals to be evaluated and to assure that the assessment of the performance of the administrator is primarily restricted to those stated expectations.

The evaluation process, as with most other aspects of superintendent-board relations is predicated on the presence of a good faith compact which is strictly adhered to by all parties. If the business of educating children is conducted by individuals of goodwill, most problems are eliminated at the outset.

SUMMARY OF EFFECTIVE EVALUATION POINTERS AND PRACTICES

- Making sure it happens regularly
- Developing clear timelines
- Creating specific performance goals

- Assuring that trust exists
- Creating a process marked by forthright dialogue

Chapter Eight

Creating An Effective Communication Program

For every breakdown in relations in a local school district there is usually a corresponding goal for improvement entitled "communication." As with so many things of this type, the problem is generally easier to identify than the solution.

For that reason, the topic of communication will be touched upon in a variety of ways, including techniques for establishing effective relations with both the staff and the community. As noted elsewhere, there is no greater barrier to effective staff performance than poor communications.

At one ESD, during the very time when budgets were at their most devastating level, the board invested heavily in a program entitled "Crucial Conversations" because of their belief communication was such an important element of more efficient and effective operational strategies.

One of the most frequent concerns of school districts considering the employment of a new administrator is the subject of communications. In situations where the search for new leadership is the outgrowth of problems, communications will often be at the heart of the matter. And as a result, boards will include expectations in their search materials which approach the need for specific skills and experiences in this area from a variety of angles. Some of these examples would include:

- "Demonstrates excellent listening and communication skills including an interest in hearing from all sides of an issue"
- "Demonstrates the ability to communicate effectively with a wide array of audiences and can process information as part of effective dialogue"

- "Has a vision of what the high school will become and the ability to articulate that vision, consider and incorporate other points of view, build consensus, and initiate change"
- "Is a good communicator with the capacity to relate to a wide variety of individuals"
- "A people person with the ability and desire to interact with staff and the community"
- "A vision for the future of education and the ability to forge a collaborative response"
- "The capacity to honor and respect divergent opinions"
- "Excellent communication and listening skills, being approachable to all staff and patrons, and able to produce clearly written communications such as newsletters, memos, and newspaper articles"
- "Has superior communication and listening skills, including the ability to write and speak in an articulate manner"
- "Demonstrates a proven record of effective communication with the Board of Education"

Ironically, while communication is generally viewed as verbalization, listening is considered to be as important an element as talking. In fact, hearing what the other person is saying may be considerably more valuable as a part of being responsive than the capacity to articulate one's own thoughts.

A budding challenge in the area of communication is the fact the age of technology has dramatically reduced the need for face-to-face conversations. And while the telephone requires direct interaction, e-mail does not.

A number of studies have suggested 93 percent of communication during a conversation or encounter is nonverbal. Both the telephone and e-mail eliminate that portion of the equation. There is growing concern about miscommunication associated with the use of e-mail. In fact, more and more organizations are encouraging either the use of some additional form of etiquette in e-mail messaging or, whenever possible, face-to-face conversations.

E-mail is easy and quick, but it can also be a path to misunderstanding.

BOARD COMMUNICATIONS

One of the first pieces of advice for any new superintendent is to make a plan for communicating with the board on a regular basis. Dr. Dennis Ray, who was superintendent of the Walla Walla School District in Washington and in the Northshore School District, also in Washington, regularly published a document entitled "The Friday Update."

Many superintendents have used something similar with different names and different formats.

The regular update is designed to provide every board member with equal access to consistent and fundamental information about what is happening in the district—what events have taken place, what the administrators are thinking about, what issues are being handled, what issues are looming, and what successes are being celebrated. Even if it's just an idea that is beginning to form, the update is a good way of "running it up the flagpole just to see if anyone salutes."

Administrators will also want to develop a special communications system for keeping board members in the loop when emergencies take place. When there is a bus accident, major student injury or death, fire, serious staff disciplinary action, or a similar event, board members want to be among the first to know the nature of the problem and what is being done.

Board members are elected to represent the community-at-large and they are expected to be aware of background information on every major issue impacting the school. Most board members do not like being caught off-guard when something major happens in the district.

INTERNAL COMMUNICATIONS

A second communication device is the internal communication piece designed to provide all staff members with equal access to basic information. The most logical time for its publication is to report the actions of the board on a timely basis.

This publication need not be lengthy. There are comprehensive examples which include recipes, funny stories, poems, illustrations, and so on, however it isn't the mission of the organization to provide reading material for its employees. The only mission in this regard is to be informative about the issues surrounding the operation of the institution. This certainly does not preclude sharing items of celebration and concern involving individual staff members. The publication should include much the same type of information that is shared with the board—what are is being worked on, what issues are being addressed, what the staff is thinking about, and what should be celebrated.

With the advent of Web sites, blogs, and similar forms of communication, a number of administrators and organizations have gone away from printed materials and are simply providing such updates on-line.

While superintendents should try to be careful about over-using the "all staff e-mail" function, there are occasions when it works to share important news with the staff through a special letter. Responses from staff members who appreciate being kept in the loop and enjoy being trusted with important agency information suggest they value being in the loop.

COMMUNICATIONS TO PARENTS

Many schools and districts publish newsletters or send some type of materials home to parents. The initial publication from a new superintendent or principal will very likely establish whether or not there will be a readership.

Many such publications include a front page "A Message From The Principal." Hopefully, not too much time is invested in the writing of such articles because a number of studies have shown that almost no time is invested on the part of readers according to several studies, including one conducted by the National School Public Relations Association.

How many times have administrators used an opening like "gee, here it is September already" or "where did the school year go." What parents want to know is who is teaching their children and what they are learning. Information about upcoming events also rates high on the list.

Perhaps the most effective communication device is a simple two-page message to parents which includes one side of printed district or building-level information including a calendar and similar useful facts. On the back side, students write a letter to their parents talking about who their teachers are and what they are studying in class.

It is easy to toss aside a district or building newsletter without reading it. Few parents are able to ignore something written to them by their children. The writing exercise also serves as a valuable contribution to the learning process.

The studies have also shown that the likelihood of the materials getting home to parents happens in reverse proportion to the age of the students. In other words, the younger the student, the more likely the material will find its way to a parent. Most high schools and many middle schools use the mail service. Elementary schools, on the other hand, can operate with some confidence that what they send home will get there even if parents have to find it in the backpack.

DISTRICT-WIDE NEWSLETTERS

The principles that impact messages from the school to the home are similar to those underlying the development of district-wide newsletters. The readership of articles entitled "From The President's Desk" or "From The Superintendent's Desk" are no more likely to be read by the community-at-large than they are by parents.

The community also has an interest in who is teaching the children, what are they being taught, how much of an impact it is making on student achievement, and what events are being held at the school. The community is also interested in knowing how the education system is interfacing with the overall community and the quality of stewardship which is being provided.

The community shares a similar interest in the individual interaction between school employees and the community in which the schools are located. This is generally not an issue among classified employees because most of them are already ingrained in the community. It is a more visible process among teachers and administrators since many of them are not ingrained.

The community probably cares more about getting to know the leaders on a social basis and certainly a personal basis than they do about what the individual is actually doing administratively or in the classroom.

It is important for administrators not to underestimate how the community feels about having its school employees living in the district as opposed to commuting from somewhere else. Particularly in small districts, community members, parents, and students, appreciate visiting with teachers at Ray's Food Center, Chester's Market, Cardinal Quik Stop, or the Rocket Café, just as much as they do seeing them at school.

Chapter Nine

Building A Foundation For Effective Relations and Understanding Rural Communities

"The fact that a local school district sees the need to replace a departing leader should not be confused with an overwhelming mandate for wholesale change in an institution "that has served us well for generations."

RURAL ECONOMICS

There are no courses on the administrative training track that address the subject of Economics 101 in Rural Communities. And yet, there is an inextricable tie between what is happening economically in small communities and in the schools that serve them.

Not the least of those issues would be the general trend of enrollment decline brought on by smaller families and vanishing job opportunities. There is also often a change in the makeup of families served by the school. In many farming communities, the schools used to serve the large families who occupied wheat farms and cattle ranches. It wasn't unusual for a farm to produce eight, ten, or even a dozen children. Now, if there are any children at all, the families are considerably smaller.

There is also a growing incidence of poverty as families search for cheaper housing options and nieces, nephews, and grandchildren come to live with relatives because of issues involving their parents. The socio-economic makeup of schools in many small communities has been changed both by the draw of cheaper housing options and the presence of children who have been sent there to live with relatives.

ECONOMIC CHALLENGES IN SMALL COMMUNITIES

Between 1969 and the year 2000, U.S. earnings per job climbed 30 percent. In Oregon, earnings per job grew by 20 percent. In rural Oregon, earnings per job remained flat during that twenty-one-year period. In most cases, those jobs have revolved around resource-based enterprises such as farming, fishing, forestry, and mining.

Rural administrators can't just focus on strategies for improving student achievement or how to manage the business affairs of a school district. They need to be aware of such other subjects as mill closings, water right battles, foreign competition, urban sprawl, rising hunger and poverty rates, and changes in the structure of families.

They also need to understand the delicate balance that exists between salaries for school staff and the community-at-large. Whereas pay scales in rural areas are based upon local supply and demand factors, salaries for school teachers and administrators are generally based upon on a broader competitive scale that includes other districts, other job opportunities, and sometimes regional or state salary schedules.

Recently, researchers at Oregon State University conducted a study of the economic factors impacting rural communities. Not surprisingly, they found that these small towns are at a disadvantage. Their research demonstrated that the more isolated, the farther from a metropolitan area, or the greater the distance a community is from a major highway, the more likely it is to suffer economic hardships.

Small towns everywhere are pretty much the same, particularly if they've been around for awhile. There's a spirit of friendliness and an aura of family while at the same time there's also something of a longing for what their town used to be when the business district wasn't boarded up or was filled with something besides second-hand stores and antique shops along with the few businesses that are able to survive even in tough times—the tavern, the post office, a small bank branch, and the utility company. If there's still a hardware store or even a pharmacy, it might well include the local liquor franchise which helps keep the business afloat. The grocery store has often been replaced by a mini-mart which also serves as the local source of gasoline.

Not every town is the same, of course. Some communities have re-invented themselves through a community development process and have managed to find a new source of identity, often as a tourist attraction or destination. Others have simply allowed the decline to advance.

CHANGES IN FAMILY LIFE

In larger areas, families have often become more far-flung, rarely living near each other. In small towns, they have managed to remain together. In larger areas, people are also separated from one another by socio-economic factors. That isn't the case in small towns where people from all economic strata generally socialize together and often live side-by-side.

Long before television, the Internet, Facebook, Twitter, I-Pods, and a host of other inventions intruded upon the simple life that used to define neighborhoods in communities of almost every size, there was a sense of communal existence in which people cared about one another, were interested in what happened around them, and invested their time in interaction with their neighbors. They used to take walks, sit on their front porches, and greet those who passed by. Now they've gone inside.

If vestiges of that sense of communal living still exist anywhere in America today, it is in small, rural communities.

ROLE OF THE SCHOOL

In many small towns, the school has become the largest single employer and as such has become something more than the educational and social center of community life. It is, for the most part, the single remaining link to a time when the town was more prosperous, when there was a greater sense of identity, and when a whole lot of things represented what is generally referred to as "the good old days."

As the largest single employer and operating with a budget far beyond that which usually exists anywhere else in town, the school has a capacity which, while difficult to define, is an important foundation in anything that happens. Those resources are often utilized in virtually all aspects of community life.

In small towns where the school has been closed, there's a hole far deeper than simply the void created by the absence of a local education system.

CONNECTING WITH THE COMMUNITY

As a result of the tie that exists between the school and the community, it should not be surprising that one of the most consistent issues in terms of criteria for the selection of new school administrators is their ability to connect with the community they serve.

Particularly in rural areas, where the school is the center of the community, how the administrator builds relationships, builds support for the school, and fits in with the community-at-large is a major concern to selection teams. Often, community members can trace their roots back many generations while the school leader may be a complete outsider. A serious part of any entry plan should be careful consideration of how to take those first steps in terms of reaching out and becoming visible and involved.

Some of the criteria which districts have used in seeking new administrators have included:

- "The ability to build support for the district through communicating effectively with all segments of the community"
- "A highly visible and accessible leadership style"
- "A proven record of open and regular communication with all stakeholders"
- "Will be an effective representative of the high school in terms of personal interactions, gathering support, creating enthusiasm, and fostering confidence"
- "Isn't afraid to become involved in community events"
- "A history of civic involvement and prior success in public relations"
- "Continue to build on the District's positive relationship with parents, city government, and community groups"
- "Has a history of developing sound and enduring relations with parents, community groups, and business or governmental leaders"
- "Understands the role of the superintendent as a key leader in the community as well as in the school"

FITTING IN

Many people relocating to long-established rural areas talk about "closed communities," or the impossibility of becoming part of a community. Like so many other issues, if one tells oneself that story regularly, it becomes a self-fulfilling prophecy. There are many examples of school administrators becoming part of a community much quicker than other new residents. First of all, the administrator is instantly an important person in the life of the community, the staff, and the students. Second, most residents understand that they are not likely to have administrators who represent a fourth or fifth generation and readily accept that fact.

> There's an old western song, which says, "pass me by, if you're only passing through." Many residents in rural communities would offer much the same advice when it comes to getting to know school administrators.

Those who genuinely start by getting the lay of the land, take stock of local issues, avoid hasty judgments, and become acquainted on a sincere level, find that they are readily accepted and welcomed. While most community members and parents respect the knowledge and training of a new administrator, they don't really care how much they know until they know how much they care.

It is a good idea to shop at home whenever possible. Those who pay the taxes to support the schools depend upon local customers. Not everything is readily available in some rural communities, but there are generally plenty of essentials, which are. In Pendleton, which has a fair-sized business district, the Chamber of Commerce says the merchants don't expect the residents to make all of their purchases in town...they only want a fair chance at their business.

It's hard to get patrons interested in ideas affecting the school without returning the favor. In farming communities, it never hurts to know when calves are up or down or the going price for a ton of alfalfa. Is the price of wheat going to hold, is enough rain falling at the right time, or how is the price of fuel impacting the bottom line? Farmers and ranchers don't expect the superintendent or principal to double as an extension agent but they do appreciate it if the administrator is at least sensitive to the market factors affecting them.

If 4-H and FFA are important to students, one of the first things the new administrator can do in August or September is to visit the local fair to check out the exhibits from the FFA Chapter and find the 4-H clubs that represent the community served by the school. A visit with the students and the parents at the exhibits would be well-received. An added bonus is a purchase at the fat stock sale. On the larger animals, it helps to find a partner or two unless one has a very large family.

VALUING WHAT YOU FIND

New administrators are wise to pick their battles carefully, no matter what needs fixing. Most schools and school districts represent a collage of all those who have passed before...and in many cases, those who remain. It is always well to demonstrate respect for what is there and what others have contributed, even if someone left under fire. Despite the circumstance, everyone will have provided something positive during his or her tenure.

> *A retired superintendent likes to tell the story of the "three envelopes." A new superintendent coming into a small, rural district asked the predecessor for some guidance. "In your desk," the retiree told him, "are three envelopes which I have prepared for you. Whenever you get into trouble, open an enve-*

> lope." Several months later, he found himself needing to open the first envelope. It read, blame the previous superintendent. He took the advice and blamed the previous superintendent. It worked. More time passed and again it came time to open an envelope so he unearthed the second missile. This one read, blame the board. And so he did and it worked, but not quite as well. More time passed and he found himself seeking out the third envelope. This one read, "prepare three envelopes."

It makes for a good story but in actual practice, it really isn't a good idea to start blaming either the previous superintendent or the board. Generally the best practice is to simply take the heat. In fact, in working with a board in their search for a superintendent, one of the board members said he hoped they would find someone who "wasn't afraid to admit a mistake and move on."

In one district, where the superintendent was the fourth to serve in a two-year period, it became quickly apparent there were a number of people around who enjoyed remaining mired in controversy and revisiting all the unhappy events that had taken place.

Finally, at the suggestion of the high school principal, a thousand fliers were printed which said simply, "don't look back unless you intend to go there." They were posted on every available wall.

That same advice has been useful in a variety of other districts. Every school setting and every community represents a strange web of beliefs, relationships, feuds, mistrust, pride, and possessiveness. Any new administrator stepping into this web is well advised to step carefully and with great sensitivity.

GETTING PARENTS INVOLVED

Most parents are anxious to be involved in the education of their children but are also pulled in a variety of directions by work schedules and other conflicts. In Oregon, as in other states, greater attention is being given to the development of an understanding of generational poverty and its implications for school administrators.

This new focus on poverty is an outgrowth of the changing socio-economic conditions facing rural communities and the change in the nature of families who occupy rural communities.

Understanding the challenges being faced by parents is critical to the equation of getting them involved. For example, holding kindergarten registration from 10 a.m. until noon on a weekday may be convenient for the school but it may not work for parents who are unable to leave their jobs to register their children.

One expert on the poverty issue talked about the challenges of homeless parents and those who might be living in cars, vans, or even camping out or living in remote shanties. For these parents, simply getting their children to school is a challenge. In response to these challenges, some schools have begun moving away from their traditional hard-line tardy policies and greetings such as "where have you been" or "one more tardy and you are out of here" to "we are happy to see you" or "we're glad you made it."

> *At a middle school that served a low-income, racially diverse clientele, one young teacher spent considerable time talking to students about the need for setting up a study area. The teacher suggested to the students that they were more likely to get quality work done at home if they would just make the effort to create an area with a desk, good lighting, and plenty of privacy—away from other family diversions. The teacher would assign the students a good measure of homework and each time the work wasn't done, would revisit the creation of the study area.*
>
> *The school principal, who had served in the area for more than a decade, became aware of the "homework/study area issue" which was beginning to cause a stir among parents. He contacted a parent with children at the school and asked if he could bring the teacher over for a visit. The parent complied with the request and the following afternoon, the principal and teacher dropped by.*
>
> *There they found a situation fairly typical in the area served by the school—a unit that offered a small kitchen, two bedrooms, and a living room. It was occupied by the parents, six children including a wife and baby belonging to the oldest son, a grandmother, and an uncle (who was recently divorced and was temporarily living with the family).*
>
> *On the way back to the school, the principal kindly asked the obvious question, "if you were going to establish the kind of study area you have asked your student to create, where in that particular house would you put it?"*

In the development of expectations for parents, it is important that their inability to provide things for their children not be confused with a sense they don't care. Even basic things like physical education uniforms, new tennis shoes, or a long list of school supplies may be more than the family can afford. Families who are preoccupied with finding their next meal or a place to live simply lack the capacity to respond in the same way as those who are living comfortably without such basic challenges.

As part of the administrative search process, parents and staff have raised questions for candidates such as:

- "What have you done to engage parents?"
- "Do you support the growing need for a stronger relationship between parents and teachers and the need to see or communicate with each other more often?"

- "Do you understand the needs of migrant parents?"
- "Do you understand the challenges of parents who are struggling to get by?"
- "What type of parent involvement models have you helped create?"
- "What types of intentional processes have you employed to involve parents?"
- "What does an effective parent involvement model look like to you?"
- "Have you ever been involved in creating a parent resource center?
- "What types of parental training activities have you been involved with?"

VISIBILITY

The topic of visibility is being covered in a variety of areas. This is because there is no word that appears more frequently in the selection process than visibility. Of all the concepts that are considered as part of the search agenda, none appears more regularly than visibility.

The first key to community relations is just that—visibility. It is also a key to student relations (and control), staff relations, and the improvement of student achievement. A school leader cannot make a meaningful or profound difference on what happens in the classroom without regular visitations.

For the sake of community relations, visibility means becoming a part of the community—not just by attending every conceivable school event, but by becoming a participant in the affairs of the community. Local service clubs are in desperate need of contributing members. In many communities, school administrators offer leadership skills that are not readily found in other occupations. As noted elsewhere, it is important to become involved in such organizations—not just by becoming a member, but by actually making a realistic contribution.

Those who are worried about sustaining a smaller community want to be assured that the school administrator is a viable part of helping make that happen. Whether they are a building principal or a superintendent, that involvement not only becomes the key to a successful relationship with the patrons, it also becomes an important foundation for building partnerships.

In some chambers of commerce, there is a belief that private businesses and schools have a different agenda. In today's educational climate it is important to become involved in all aspects of community life and help make sure that agenda becomes a common mission. For educators, there is inherent value in having a vibrant and progressive business community and it pays dividends to take the time to become involved in activities such as the chamber of commerce or other groups dedicated to economic development.

One district said it this way in sharing their expectations with prospective candidates: "Is willing to perpetuate the critical role of the schools in terms of forging an economic partnership with the community"

LIVING IN THE COMMUNITY

There is a growing number of families where both parties may be involved in school administration. At the same time, there are also a growing number of systems demanding that key administrators live in the district—not just superintendents, but principals as well. There have been searches where candidates have had to disqualify themselves as finalists because they could not meet the board's expectations for becoming full-time residents.

Just a few years ago, residency wasn't always mentioned in search brochures. Now there are statements such as:

- "An understanding of small schools and small communities and the desire to become an active participant in all phases of life in Cove, preferably including the maintenance of a residence."
- "Willingness to reside in the district and become an active, visible member of the community.
- "The principal will be expected to reside within the boundaries of the School District."
- "Wants to be a part of the Spray community as well as the Spray School District."
- "Establish permanent and primary residence in the District and be an active member of the community by being open, accessible, and connected with parents, patrons, and students."

Some districts have modified their stance just a bit, suggesting the administrator needs to readily accessible to the district and available to handle emergencies in the district as they arise.

INTERACTING WITH EVERYONE

Another of the terms that comes up often regarding potential new hires is whether or not they are approachable. In some districts, the "open door policy" is a common term. In one search brochure this was described as "excellent communication skills, being visible, approachable, and willing to listen. An articulate spokesperson for the district, the school community, and for educational issues." The same brochure talked about "a people person, with the ability and desire to interact with staff and the community."

In one recent search, where the departing superintendent was enormously popular, the individuals providing the initial input were asked to describe the most valuable characteristic of the individual who was being replaced. The overriding response was "he talked to everyone and listened to them intently."

They went on to note, "he didn't just 'hangout' at ball games or school events with the board members or a few cronies. He constantly circulated and was willing to talk to any parent, student, or community member with whom he came in contact. People liked that, he didn't appear to think he was anyone special."

That particular district contained three different types of parents and citizens—the orchardists, packers, and other residents who had been there for generations, the escapees from a nearby city of 70,000 who had built glitzy new homes along the rim of the valley, and the migrant farm workers whose children now made up half of the student enrollment. Every one of them got the attention of the superintendent.

A WELCOMING IMAGE

Parking spaces make a statement about who is important. If the best two spots are reserved for the principal and secretary, this speaks volumes. Budding administrators are encouraged to find a business downtown where the most accessible spots are set aside for the owner rather than customers.

At a country club in Eastern Oregon, the two prime parking spots at the main entrance are on either side of the front sidewalk. One has a large sign that says "reserved for club manager", the other has a sign which says, "reserved for club pro." The members, many of whom are elderly, are reminded each time they arrive, just where they stand.

ENGAGEMENT OF NON-PARENTS

In a growing number of communities, the population without children attending school is generally the majority. That's why it makes sense to reach out to that population and engage them in the educational process. It also makes sense to make schools community or neighborhood centers that play an important part in the social life of the community. Whenever possible, school events should be open to as many citizens as possible. School facilities should be made available for use by community groups so that they develop a sense of ownership by frequenting the schools and district offices. The potential profit from renting school facilities is fairly minimal so unless events are being conducted as private businesses or for profit, efforts should be made to open the schools as much as possible to community use. The goodwill, which results from such gestures, pays big dividends.

KEEPING UP THE APPEARANCE OF THE FACILITIES

Knowing the vast majority of the citizens in the community do not have students in school, it is well to remember that many of them will judge the quality of management by what they see when they drive by or what the building looks like when they come to some kind of an event.

Whether it's a new building or an old one, it can still be kept up. One time a principal whose school was on a busy road suggested the maintenance department take a look at the eaves on the end of her building, which was by the road. She pointed out that the paint had worn off and that it was clearly visible to anyone driving by. It took about an hour of maintenance time and a small amount of paint to change the appearance.

Even in the summer, it is worth the effort to mow the grass and get rid of the weeds. Junk should not be allowed to pile up, even in out-of-the-way areas. Once the clutter starts, it builds on itself. Even though money is tight and maintenance often gets cut, the community does not immediately assume that shoddy appearance is a necessary outgrowth of budget problems.

Taxpayers expect the school personnel to be good stewards of what they have been provided...no matter how old or meager it might be. Some administrators use creativity in finding ways to get flowers planted and new shrubs installed. They can be equally creative in finding ways to get junk hauled off...despite the rules on surplus property.

School events should be treated as if company is coming because in fact the school is hosting very important guests. Sometimes it becomes necessary to have the students help with the preparations because the custodial staff can't always totally cover the classrooms. If all the paper in a room is picked up and some effort has been made, it makes the custodial work more feasible. It isn't unrealistic to ask students to leave a room in the same condition that they found it.

There's a very old elementary school in Dayton, Oregon where the floors glisten, the entryway is well-marked and neat, the walls are neatly covered with student work, the paint is fresh, and it is clear that this is a school which, despite its age, had been well-cared for. It made a tremendous first impression and it also made it clear that this was a district which was well-managed and which takes pride in its facilities.

Many schools spend a good deal of time and effort talking about school pride or district pride. Despite the slogans and the public relations, appearances speak louder than words.

TRADITIONS

New administrators will want to become aware of traditions as quickly as possible, whether they are specific to a particular building, a district, or the community-at-large. They might want to ask questions such as what are the events and activities that an individual school has historically conducted? Or, what did the former administrator do in terms of events or activities for the staff?

Perhaps the previous principal served breakfast to the staff as a source of appreciation on the last day of school. It's good to know that this has happened and to be able to make a conscious decision about its perpetuation rather than experience an oversight.

Maybe the previous principal took each teacher's class for half a day or perhaps they operated a committee of veteran teachers who met to help decide on the school's annual major supply order.

It would also be advisable to find out if the previous principal had annoying practices that the staff would just as well see end.

At the district or community level, new administrators would be well-advised to learn as quickly as possible about the major events are in the community…and to become involved and visible. In one town, it was traditional for the school administrators to chair and organize the annual Cheese Days Parade. The files were literally passed from one new administrator to the next even though the event itself was sponsored by the Lion's Club.

There's no substitute for the importance of showing up at the St. Patrick's Day in Heppner, the Muddy Frogwater Festival in Milton-Freewater, Caledonian Days in Athena-Weston, the Festival of Trees Auction or the Farm-City Pro Rodeo in Hermiston, the Echo Boosters Golf Tournament, or whatever is important to the local community.

Chapter Ten

Building a Foundation For Effective Staff Relations

THE ZEAL FOR CHANGE MAY NOT BE PERVASIVE

Eager new principals and superintendents are generally more zealous about their new assignments than the people they are about to supervise. In fact, many of those they are about to meet are actually in place to assure the status quo—either consciously or subconsciously. Even in cases where the staff enthusiastically embraces a change of leadership, it's good to remember they aren't the ones who just landed a new job. This is why all others have a diminished level of interest in the concept of change or why they aren't stricken with the same sense of new opportunity.

A California study designed to help frame support for new principals found that new principals sometimes have to spend an inordinate amount of time coping with old baggage that was left behind or a climate in which they become so preoccupied putting out fires they don't have time to consider the more important issues. Sometimes a building climate is almost designed to preoccupy the administrator with the mundane.

As noted, the principal generally possesses a stronger commitment to change than does the staff. Beyond just a lack of zeal, it is sometimes possible to encounter some level of sabotage from veterans who perceive themselves running the school and don't want to give that up.

In some cases they don't believe they have anything to learn. In others, they almost make a sport out of running off new leaders. While these cases may be isolated, new principals should enter with their eyes open and realize that some of these veterans may have extensive community connections, strong parental support, and close ties with one or more board members.

The same is true for superintendents. Most major program shifts require a span of at least four to six years. Many in the system realize that with a revolving door in the superintendent's office, major changes in the school environment and dramatic upgrades in expectations can be avoided.

In one district, the board secretary and the business manager had wielded major influence during a span of time that included multiple superintendent changes. Along the way, they had gathered a cadre of community members and employees who were supportive of their cause.

An outside examination of the situation revealed significant glitches in business practices, overreporting of funds that were due the district, inconsistencies in staff compensation, and oversights that caused hardships for staff members.

As the superintendent and board sought to remedy the situation, they were met with strong resistance from those who were reluctant to relinquish their power base. Despite the obvious need for change in order to comply with state and federal guidelines, as well as good business practices, the new superintendent experienced what could best be described as a nightmare as he sought to right the ship and provide stability for the district.

Even in the face of growing enrollment, enhanced parental involvement, rising test scores, and a much more compatible relationship with employee groups, there continued to be strong resistance based upon efforts to retain a long-standing power base.

STAFF DEVELOPMENT

In one rural Idaho district, the whole staff goes on a retreat versus the traditional administrative retreat, which is the trademark of larger school districts—a luxury that would, for the most part, be logistically impossible with a staff numbering in the hundreds or thousands. Luxury, however, is not the trademark of the council plan—they spend the day at a youth camp talking about goals, getting to know each other better, and establishing a mutual focus for the district.

EVALUATION AND SUPERVISION

One of the critical challenges facing new administrators is crossing the bridge from being part of the rank-and-file to being in charge. It is amazing how much energy is sometimes devoted to attempts to remain "one of the gang." While new administrators don't need to go to great lengths to "wear their stripes," it is at least well to come to grips with the fact that things have changed and that the term "it's lonely at the top" begins to have real meaning.

At the same time, while it is important to accept the transformation from one of the gang to a new role, new administrators would be well-advised to wear the new mantle of responsibility with a sense of humility. This is particularly important in a field like education where the ranks of the staff are filled with highly-educated individuals with complex skills and interests.

> One budding leader-type took a new employee around the building for a personal introduction to the staff. Each time she made the introduction, she said, "I would like you to meet so-and-so, she will be reporting directly to me and I will be her supervisor." True leaders are both humble and rarely have the need to make a show out of waving their stripes. The effort at making the introductions was certainly thoughtful, but unfortunately the value of the exercise was overshadowed by the power trip.

One of the more difficult challenges will be evaluating personnel and with that, perhaps telling people things that they don't wish to hear. In many cases, the person doing the telling is more concerned about the impact than the person on the receiving end.

In an era in which education will be charged with the mission of doing more with less, and with accelerated expectations for student achievement, the role of the principal as an instructional leader will expand. Studies of the most effect practices for improving student achievement often relate the importance of holding high expectations for staff, the development of goals, and rigorous attention to what is going on in the classrooms including monitoring student progress and instructional interventions.

All of this leads to an effective evaluation system and the creation of quality dialogue between the administrator and the classroom teacher. The evaluation system ought not be confused with the need to occasionally provide teachers with commendations. Good principals will write memos or notes to good teachers applauding their effectiveness or specific accomplishments. This practice allows them to separate the letter writing from the assessment process and to then be able to complete the evaluation document itself with a strong focus on the criteria.

In the end, as in the evaluation of superintendents and principals, the same three words most likely to guide the effective evaluation of staff and most other staff-related issues will be fairness, trust, and consistency.

Chapter 10
HANDLING STAFF ISSUES INDIVIDUALLY

Early in his career, a principal took the occasion at one faculty meeting to discuss a growing problem with punctuality and slipping out early. Rather than addressing the individual culprits, he chose to discuss the problem universally with the entire staff, which must have felt like a much safer approach.

Following the meeting, a veteran staff member stopped by his office and said, "I have never been late to school in my entire career and I have never left the building early for inappropriate reasons. I find it very offensive to be addressed with this concern since it does not pertain to me. You might be better served to take up such matters with the responsible individuals rather than condemning the entire staff." It takes considerably more courage to confront individual staff members than it does the entire group but it is a more logical and effective approach.

There are lots of thoughts around the concept of treating staff members as professionals. In a perfect world, licensed staff members will give well beyond the limitations of their basic contract. Many classified staff members would like to be but they are bound by limitations on the time they can spend outside of regular working hours. An administrator who wishes to foster a climate in which staff members want to be professional and go above and beyond must begin by demonstrating the trust and the flexibility that creates the right conditions for this to occur.

> *One time a young administrator was called to the superintendent's office in June and asked to provide a comprehensive calendar of his work schedule for the year. The superintendent told the young administrator he wanted to make sure he had put in the required number of days. After completing the calendar, the administrator discovered he had worked an extra thirteen days.*
>
> *That afternoon, he purchased a plane ticket and flew to California for two weeks.*
>
> *In the process he advised his supervisor he assumed if they were concerned about whether or not he had worked enough days, there would be equal concern about having worked too many days. It was a somewhat gutsy move that might not have been received as well as it was.*
>
> *In the end, it proved to be a learning experience for both parties. The supervisor later told the young administrator the incident suggested that preoccupation with time schedules for people in key positions probably doesn't have much relationship to whether or not they are getting the job done and that most administrators who are doing a good work way beyond their contracts. For those who don't get the job done, that fact becomes evident in many ways beside the time card.*

THE VISIBLE LEADER

Visibility may well be one of the most common themes in searches for new administrators—students, staff, parents, and community members want a school leader who is seen on a regular basis. Several excerpts from the search process help highlight what boards and communities are looking for in principals and superintendents. These include:

- "Creates unity and respect through consistent and just practices in all relationships"
- "A willingness to be highly-visible in the community, in the classrooms, and at school events"
- Will be visible at literally everything that happens in the schools and the community—including a willingness to be visible in the classrooms supporting teachers and students and observing the learning process."

A common error of school administrators is spending too much time out of the district or school building. Often principals and superintendents find it easier to schedule attendance at meetings or other events that take them to other locations and yet they have difficulty scheduling themselves out in buildings or classrooms for long periods of time.

Perhaps no other single act of an administrator can have as much positive impact than being visible and involved in the school, the district, and the community. Certainly the time spent in classrooms observing what is taking place can provide multiple benefits. It never hurts for parents at the dinner table to be reminded by their children that the principal was in their classroom that day.

And, when parents are calling with concerns about a staff member, it is helpful if the administrator can respond based upon a litany of personal observations.

SELECT EFFECTIVE LEADERS

As one retired superintendent noted:

> "The two people who are most likely to get you fired are the business manager and the high school principal."

Both are critical positions and often are some of the most difficult to fill. It is also true that the most likely source of major problems is the business office and the high school. However, even knowing that, every leadership position in the district is critical. As schools become leaner in this area, the need for quality leadership becomes even more acute.

Every hour spent chasing references will pay off in the end. A wise district will leave no stone unturned in its search for background information prior to hiring a new administrator. And, whenever possible, a site visit is an effective way of adding confidence to the decision.

Interviews provide some information about the kind of staff relations which are characteristic of candidates, but actually visiting with those they supervise and work with on a regular basis can yield considerable helpful information.

EMPOWERING OTHERS

> "I won't tell you what plays to call, but I might suggest that you not call that same play again."
>
> Former WSU Head Football Coach Bill Doba
> (In a message to his assistant coaches)

In conducting searches, consultants work with the board, staff, administration, parents, and the community in determining the challenges and demands of the specific position and the qualifications and qualities which are desired in the new administrator. While the composite of the information is unique to each district, there are some central themes that have emerged on a regular basis.

The concept of delegation and the empowerment of staff is one of the most frequent concepts put forth by all parties within the education equation. Empowerment or delegation seem like simple goals to achieve. However, effectively using this concept requires considerable self-confidence and the ability to deal with ambiguity. It also includes a clear understanding of how to franchise employees while also providing the necessary support and tools to get the job done.

Some years ago, a business executive named Robert Townsend wrote a book entitled *"Up The Organization"*. Townsend was the individual who built Avis into a power within the rental car business with his "We Try Harder" campaign. Although hundreds of books have since appeared based on the concept of valuing employees, Townsend's book was clearly one of the first. Bizarre as it might seem as a concept today, several generations ago it was not uncommon for supervisors to remind employees "we hired you from the head down."

In his book, Townsend offered such thoughts as "the good leader carries water to the workers so that they can get on with the job" or "the old leader wants all of the medals, the new leader passes them out and finds the most satisfaction rejoicing in the success of others."

The empowerment of staff is exactly what Townsend was talking about. Today's workers want to be part of the action and they want to be empowered in their work. In fact, there are those who will make major career choices based upon their capacity to make a difference or a profound impact—and that doesn't generally happen without empowerment.

In looking through past administrative search materials, the concept of empowerment and valuing employees was phrased in various ways. Here are some examples:

- "Empowers staff members and promotes ownership"
- "Has demonstrated an administrative style which includes equity for all staff members"
- "A leadership style characterized by the empowerment of others"
- "Possesses the ability to empower, inspire, and acknowledge the accomplishments of the staff"
- "An appreciation for the contribution of others"
- "A track record of displaying genuine respect for every employee and valuing everyone's contribution to serving the needs of children and youth"
- "A reputation for valuing the thoughts, ideas, and contributions of every individual employee in the school district"
- "Offers a leadership style characterized by inspiration, motivation, and the empowerment of others"
- "The skills to lead and motivate a highly-competent staff through collaboration, delegation, and accountability."

Mixed in with the concept of empowerment is valuing the worth and contribution of every employee. School districts have typically had a hierarchy built with the teachers as the experts and classified employees relegated to a position sometimes viewed as "second-class citizens." This is a term which comes up often in search work and in the conduct of management reviews for local school districts. Those who drive the buses, balance the books, handle the secretarial duties, clean and maintain the buildings, and feed the students want to be acknowledged for their contributions to the educational process.

Principals and superintendents who view their role as facilitating and valuing the work of these individuals will find that they are capable of achieving far more than anyone imagined. The key to survival in small schools is the creative empowerment of others. In one district, which suddenly found itself with one administrator instead of two, it became necessary to divide up the jobs among staff members. What they found was interesting. It was also a district with a low salary schedule and some of the ambitious young staff members were delighted with the stipends for such things as athletic director, program director, etc., Five thousand dollars makes a big difference to someone making $35,000 a year.

In the course of trying to figure out how to get the work done with limited help and resources, agencies sometimes overlook assets they already have at their disposal including human capital. For some school districts, that capital comes in the form of classified employees who are being under-utilized.

These are individuals who may have hidden talents and capabilities that have never been recognized. Much of the underlying philosophy behind this initiative can be found in the simple willingness of a school or school district to give these employees a chance. Just telling someone "you believe in them" can often set them on a course to dramatic new contributions to the organization.

Chapter Eleven

Maintenance and Facilities

THE IMAGE

There are many reasons why the appearance of the school makes an important statement. In some communities, as many as three-fourths of the residents do not have children attending school and in many cases, those individuals have little, if any reason to ever visit the inside of the school.

As a result, their image of how well the school is managed is often based upon what they see when they drive by. If what they see is litter on the school grounds, peeling paint, weeds, and general signs of neglect, they assume that the school is not being well-managed and that the taxpayer investment in school facilities is being left to neglect.

School administrators ought not assume that because funds are tight, the community is understanding about neglected facilities. They simply assume that the funds are not being spent properly. The basics of making sure schools look attractive are not necessarily high cost items.

> *Dayton Elementary School, which was mentioned earlier, is probably somewhere in the vicinity of seventy years old but its age is not immediately obvious to the average visitor except for the fact that it has the architectural look of a school from that vintage.*
> *The outside of the school is clean and neat. The shrubs, lawn, and planted areas show signs of pride and attention. Inside, the floors are polished and shiny and the walls are brightly painted. Student work is displayed neatly up and down the halls.*
> *Everyone in the school seemed to be committed to the idea of school pride and the offices and classrooms reflected the same kind of attention to an orderly learning environment that was bright and cheery.*

Managing school facilities and even individual classrooms is not unlike taking care of one's personal home. Once the first old car is left in a field next to the house or an old washer or dryer is stacked next to the garage, the second, third, and fourth come more easily.

Schools, reluctant to go through the hassle of surplusing unused items, keep things around that haven't been used in years. The accumulation is a waste of valuable space inside and outside of the school as well as in individual classrooms. It is also blight on the image of the school.

> *Another school deserving of commendation is the North Lake School near Fort Rock, Oregon This is a newer building but one that is considerably older than it looks.*
> *The building simply radiates an image of pride and care. As in Dayton, the halls literally gleam and everything is in place. When asked why the school looked so well-maintained, the board and administration simply noted that since the school was the center of the entire community, it had just always been a very high priority to make sure that it was kept in immaculate condition. Since it is such a high priority, students and staff automatically do their part to help maintain the tradition.*

THE MAINTENANCE REVIEW

About six months after the Ione School District was formed, the Facility and Grounds Committee conducted a complete walk-through along with the site administrator, the head custodian, the superintendent, and the facility consultant. In addition, staff members were asked to identify anything in their area that needed attention. Custodians also made a list. The items ranged everywhere from needing new boilers and bleachers to a broken drinking fountain or a lock that might need attention.

Once the list was complete, the tasks were divided up among a variety of individuals. Several local residents who were off during the winter and interested in doing odd jobs were hired by the hour to work down the list. At one point, during the holiday break, there were seven people working in the building. A reference list would include:

Loyal Burns: a local resident licensed to do electrical work and assorted other projects. Loyal is on-call to the district at a set rate.

Tom Brandon: a retired school administrator who is an expert on school facilities and who is retained by the district as a consultant as was Bob DePoe who helped oversee completion of the new elementary school

Maintenance: This includes the custodians as well as several local residents who agreed to work part-time for the district helping with various repairs including **Mark Bruno,** the mayor of Ione at the time. The others were paid by the hour to address the items on the list.

Kelly Griffith: head custodian
George Murdock: then the interim superintendent
Dick Allen: then the site administrator
John Rietmann/Gregg Rietmann: the two board members who were the Facilities & Grounds Committee

The results of the walk-through produced a long list of items that needed attention. The list is being included in its entirety to demonstrate the comprehensive nature of the project. Six months after the list was created, every item identified during the walk-through had been addressed.

As one might expect, a number of the items on the list had been problems for years. Being a small district, Ione was in no position to maintain a permanent staff to handle maintenance issues. The creation of a short-term maintenance team—at a relatively low cost—enabled the district to fix, repair, or replace every single item that was in need of attention. It also provided a short-term source of employment for local citizens who needed something to occupy their time.

The district will continue with its walk-through concept every six months although it is quite unlikely that it will ever be necessary to create such a long list of items needing attention.

Immediate Repair List
Move mirror in North Hall boys bathroom and paint—Maintenance
Base molding in gym under and around mats—Maintenance
Cover steam pipe in gym—Maintenance
Repair gym bleachers—Maintenance
Check, replace bulbs in all exterior lights—Kelly
Check clothes dryer operation Maintenance
Build step in boiler room to electrical panel Maintenance
Put grate back on stage wall—Maintenance
Repair benches in cafeteria—Maintenance
Replace mirror in boys bathroom (Dick will order)—Maintenance
Fill in holes in wall in library—Maintenance
Repair exhaust fan in Room 5—Maintenance
US flag and holder for cafeteria—Dick
Work with city on new water meter vault by plaza—Dick
Repair trash compacter—Maintenance
Large video screens installed in cafeteria/elem gym—Maintenance
Eliminate clutter in classrooms—Dick
Cleanup stage area—Dick

Install lip in entrances to elementary shower stalls—Maintenance
Take down cover over north side gym windows—Maintenance
Heater for shop classroom—Bob
Repair heat exchangers in North Hall and high school hall—Bob
Mailboxes in front of Plaza—Mark
Art room and Spanish room modifications—Tom
Cabinet doors for new classrooms—Tom
Window replacements—Tom
Plaza project—Tom/George
Gymnasium sound baffles—Tom
Parking area modifications—John/Gregg
Elementary gym sound system—Dick
Privacy panels—Tom
Softfall for playground—John/Gregg/Loyal
Downtown outdoor sign—George
High school locker room vents—Bob
Repair fence by swimming pool, dugouts, shop—Maintenance
Order and install new slide for playground equipment—Dick
New gate for north hall—Dick
Repair door on garage in vehicle lot—Maintenance

Electrical:
Repair lights in north crawl space/stage—Loyal
Fix light fixtures in custodial closet—Loyal
Replace exterior light on top of cafeteria—Loyal
Wire new scoreboards—Loyal
Get electricity to outside juice machine—Loyal
Repair electric heaters in main shop—Loyal
Repair exhaust fan in Room 5—Loyal
Repair trash compacter—Loyal

Locks & Doors:
New lock for doors between high school locker rooms—Maintenance
Door closure on stage door—Maintenance
Panic hardware for high school gym door—Maintenance
East cafeteria door won't lock—Maintenance
Replace lock on custodial door—Maintenance
Get door and lock system working on outside stage door—Maintenance

Plumbing:
Fix drain in Room 1—Maintenance
Connect hot water heater in Room 5—Maintenance
Fix leaky faucet in shop—Maintenance
Turn down thermostat on hot water in shop—Maintenance
Repair drinking fountain in shop—Maintenance
Repair drinking fountain in girls locker room—Maintenance

Install refrigerated drinking fountain—Maintenance
Water softener for boiler—Maintenance
Other Items/Maintenance-Custodial:
Put together new teacher desks
Put together new chairs
Install TV and video brackets on classroom walls
Assemble new butcher paper racks
Build brackets for ladders
Repair snow blower
Repair locks on front door of high school
Assemble ball carts
Repair icemaker on stage
Clean roof drains
Remove partition wall on stage
Install water filter on air lines for compressor in shop
Replace two sink faucets in Room 1
Replace one sink faucet in Room 5
Replace steam pipe in HS girls locker room

The district had not invested in equipment for maintaining the outside of the school facilities. The City of Ione purchased a new $30,000 mower and the district contracted for mowing and watering services using city employees at a fraction of what it might take to either hire regular staff or to purchase and maintain equipment.

When the district has need of tractors or similar items of equipment, community members and board members who serve on the Facility and Grounds Committee bring in the necessary equipment from their farms or private businesses.

Chapter Twelve

Fiscal Management

Budding administrators typically prefer to gravitate toward the topics of curriculum and instruction rather than budget or personnel. And districts often overlook the latter two concepts in favor of curriculum-related issues.

Certainly the ability to provide instructional leadership is a vital key to success, but so too are the people issues and the capacity to marshal the necessary resources to get the job done.

Many young administrators have discovered that by effectively managing their fiscal resources, discovering more cost-effective practices, finding new sources of funding, and monitoring their budgets, they are more likely to be able to advance their initiatives.

As part of the entry plan, it is advisable to make friends with the business manager or the deputy clerk and understand their world. They can be a real source of help and insight. They can also provide additional strategies or insights into how to expand the resource base.

One of the great contradictions in public education today is the demand to do more with less. At a time when teachers are overburdened with rising demands and declining resources, they welcome leadership that expands the resource base. Energetic administrators will pursue grants and other special sources of funding in order to help teachers achieve their objectives.

Administrators often overlook the importance that resources can play in helping achieve their goals except to worry about what the Legislature or the district aren't providing. They also overlook becoming familiar with outside resources that can play a part. Only a handful of the administrators working in districts served by an education service district actually take the time to carefully examine every possible service or support that the ESD might offer—services that can also expand the resource base.

Chapter 12
LEARN THE BUDGET

Even though most new administrators will have completed a course in school finance, one of their first areas of attention ought to be the budget. Building principals will want to study both the building budget and the district budget. Superintendent/principals will want to also study the entire district budget and become familiar with the current plan of resource allocation.

New administrators will actually want to examine the budget document line by line and make sure that they understand each entry and its purpose. Many budgets include line items that have existed for years and which have simply been perpetuated even though no one remembers the original purpose. Board members are impressed when new administrators are able to quickly identify ways of cutting costs or finding revenues already at the disposal of the district.

> *During a superintendent/principal search, the board members made a specific point of talking about the practice of simply perpetuating budget figures from one year to the next without taking the time to actually examine the purpose of the proposed expenditure.*
>
> *The board members made it clear that they wanted a candidate who knew enough about finance and had the interest to go through the budget thoroughly enough to examine the value of each and every proposed amount. It was their belief that such an examination of the resources would help align expenditures with priorities and probably result in the discovery of extra funds that might be available.*

Many new building-level administrators will be coming to their positions from the classroom and therefore will be focused on instruction and issues related to teaching. One of the greatest contributions they can make toward improved instruction and enhancing classroom opportunities is to acquire the skills to manage the budget in such a way that resources can be maximized.

EXPLORE NEW SOURCES OF REVENUE

Adversity sometimes results in opportunity and the difficult fiscal challenges facing schools can become the impetus to look at new funding sources or ways to make cuts that might otherwise be difficult to make. Sometimes it takes a recession or a dramatic downturn in the economy to force consideration of new ways of doing business that reduce costs in some areas and permit the flow of more of the remaining resources into classrooms.

In Morrow County, the citizens formed a recreation district to help offset the costs of extra-curricular activities. As a result, the local schools received over $400,000 a year for the conduct of sports, music, drama, and similar programs. Ione, for example, with 160 students, received over $80,000. This is about equal to the cost of two teaching positions. With a staff of eleven licensed personnel, this makes a major difference.

New administrators would be wise to begin treating their assignment as a business and begin to identify alternative sources of revenue to fund as many expenditure areas as possible. At first, it doesn't seem like there is much that fits into this category. However, once the spirit of entrepreneurialism begins to take shape, the pieces begin to fall into place much more naturally.

In the case of grants, the use of foundation funds, or other outside resources, it is valuable to find ways of paying for what is already happening instead of just adding new fiscal demands. Both the concept of finding loose revenue within existing budgets or finding new sources of funds to pay for what is already happening is likely to produce better results than hoping for new allocations from state or federal sources as is noted in the next chapter.

CAREFULLY EXAMINING PAST EXPENDITURE PRACTICES

It was already noted that very possibly the least likely source of new funds is state allocations. Expanding on the concept of mining for dollars among existing resources, new administrators would be wise to carefully study past practices in terms of budget expenditures with an eye toward possible savings and changes of practice.

As noted, the easiest money to find isn't new funds, but rather money that already exists in the budget that could be better used for other purposes. A new principal or superintendent ought to conduct a personal audit or value engineering exercise on current budget plans and past practices to see if there aren't ways to unearth new funds.

A number of school districts in Eastern Oregon have formed a food-purchasing cooperative in order to save money on their orders. As a result, they have cut food costs by about one fourth. Many districts have also limited their expenditures to the use of purchasing cooperatives rather than having staff members shopping individually through catalogs. Some rural districts have reported savings of 40-60 percent on the cost of supplies, instructional materials, and equipment by simply moving toward the idea of competitive bidding practices.

Even figuring out ways to consolidate athletic contests can potentially result in transportation savings as well as supervision costs and other expenses associated with conducting these activities. In the Myrtle Point and

Coquille Districts in Southwest Oregon, whenever the two schools have groups of students headed in the same direction for athletic contests or other events, they share a bus in order to cut costs. This was instituted by a new superintendent and has proven very popular with the board.

Old habits are hard to break and it takes some perseverance to make savings transpire. Sometimes providing those who discover the savings with an opportunity to share in the rewards (through added budget capacity) helps spur the enthusiasm level. People like to buy where they have always bought, they like to deal with certain salespeople, or they simply like to conduct business in a certain way. Worst of all, they might be used to receiving some type of gifts or rewards for their purchases. With diminishing resources, and in view of most state purchasing laws, those habits need breaking.

LEARNING TO WRITE GRANTS

A number of schools have augmented their coffers by writing grants. Sometimes, grant-writing assistance is available through the ESD or another source. The Stanfield and Echo School Districts in Eastern Oregon, both relatively small in size, wrote technology grants that were funded at the rate of about $200,000 each. Echo also wrote a facilities grant that resulted in about $330,000 in special funds to help with badly needed repairs.

The Yoncalla School District in Southwest Oregon wrote a lighting grant to the state which resulted in an allocation of $160,000.

Smaller grants also make a big difference. In the Milton-Freewater District in northeast Oregon, two complete computer labs were received through grant applications written to a large computer company. One of the local school buildings in Milton-Freewater received a grant to fund a summer reading program and a grant to augment library purchases by $5,000. Ione landed a $2,000 grant to help fund expanded parent involvement.

UTILIZE ALL AVAILABLE SERVICES

As noted earlier, staff at the education service district are always amazed by the inconsistency in assistance requests between districts. While some districts have carefully analyzed the range of services offered by the ESD and have sought to utilize every possible program of support, others haven't bothered to even learn what might be available.

As a result, some buildings and districts have received thousands of dollars worth of support while other districts have simply not availed themselves of programs and services that are there for the taking. In the Fall of 2003, several new principals in the area actually came to the ESD and involved themselves in a lengthy orientation and tour in order to learn all they could about what might be available to them. They have then followed this up by taking advantage of what they learned.

The ESD isn't the only agency available to provide assistance. There are also social service agencies that provide services which could be easily utilized by schools and which might result in savings.

Sometimes administrators avoid exploring these outside sources and possibilities in an effort to maintain local control. As funds become tighter, those who have created a greater sense of fiscal stability by pulling out all the stops in terms of enhancing their revenues, will enjoy a greater capacity for local control.

CREATING A FOUNDATION

Every community has a group of citizens who would prefer to give to their local schools rather than sharing their resources with more anonymous charities. Local education foundations are becoming popular as an avenue for the receipt of funds to support various aspects of the school.

Rather than simply giving to a large charity, citizens can participate in the purchase of books and other instructional materials used by their neighbors. In Ione, the education foundation provided funds so the district didn't have to split a class at the elementary level. In Heppner, another Eastern Oregon district, the education foundation provided a half-time mathematics teacher.

Education foundations can also gather funds for scholarships, to help fund staff training, to offset the costs of field trips, to buy playground equipment, or for a host of other expenditures that benefit the school program.

In some cases, particularly at the building level, some citizens like to give for identified causes. This might include buying coats for needy students, buying a specific group of books and perhaps having their contribution acknowledged inside, helping landscape part of the grounds, or providing for other specific causes. In one case, a school library expanded its collection and encouraged students to read by putting a sticker inside donated books which read "this book was donated by Harriet Stedman in order to help students at Pleasant View Elementary School become better readers."

Chapter Thirteen

Human Resources and Negotiations

A NEW BACKDROP

Closely aligned with the importance of good staff relations is the importance of understanding issues in the realm of human resource management and negotiations. In small districts, there is usually an administrator assigned specifically to this function, so much of the work falls on superintendents and principals.

The importance of understanding contracts and personnel issues almost goes without saying. It is the underpinning of effective staff relations and a key to avoiding the human relations pitfalls that can impede a successful operation. Recently, because of declining revenue and resources in many rural districts, superintendent/principals have found themselves having to make many difficult decisions.

In some extreme circumstances, there are districts where the superintendent left because of fallout from having to address severe cutbacks. Obviously schools are a fragile environment where each decision must be made with consideration for political fallout, fiscal implications, instructional concerns, and empathy for the individuals involved.

In one case, the enrollment dropped from 300 to 180 in a district but the staffing levels had remained essentially the same. The new superintendent/principal was forced to make some very difficult decisions about cutting back staff—in at least one case a very popular, but less senior staff member. Problems arose in the community and with the remaining staff who were unwilling to accept the need to reduce staff.

The board chair, who also operates a business in town, stepped down from the board because of the impact the board's decisions were having on her business. While in a philosophical way most of those involved in the process probably understood the financial problems accompanying the declining enrollment and the shortage of funds from the state and other traditional sources (in this case a well-funded ESD), a high frustration level exists in many rural communities on various economic fronts and the problems at the school get the brunt of their attention because they are generally more tangible.

In another district, the small teacher's association has been at loggerheads over negotiations and several key procedures. The need to cut staff positions became a community issue because many of the employees whose jobs are on the line are rooted in a community which is already suffering from an extraordinarily high unemployment rate caused by declines in agriculture and the timber industry. In this case, the superintendent/principal actually "grew up" on the staff, but the morale issues caused by the need to reduce staff and balance the budget have made his employment situation untenable.

In a third district, a very remote district with almost no feasible cooperative or sharing possibilities, the enrollment has dropped from about 140 down to 70 or 80 with the possibility of further declines on the horizon. Again, the district was struggling with efforts to provide a basic curriculum with a declining staff. The superintendent/principal finally left in hopes that someone else would take over the district—perhaps even in a contracted situation—because they cannot afford to pay the cost of local leadership. This is a veteran school leader with forty years of experience, but little in the way of preparation to handle the staff unrest and frustration which is essentially beyond his control.

In a fourth situation, the superintendent/principal has managed to maintain good staff relations despite the severe declines in enrollment and resources. However, his wife has also been a member of the staff and it has become necessary to eliminate her position because of the fiscal issues. They are seeking employment elsewhere in hopes that both will be able to find new jobs.

As revenues decline and expectations accelerate, both boards and administrators are struggling with the disconnect that seems to exist between a belief public agencies need to "tighten their belts" and "operate like a business" and the fact this results in reductions in programs and staff.

Board recalls, community unrest, and frequent administrative turnover become the result.

A side issue is the fact staff cuts often involve the newest and most popular or capable teachers which adds to the dilemma. In addition, these are often the staff who are handling many of the extracurricular assignments.

The problem of eliminating new staff has become such an issue that in the Fall of 2010, Secretary of Education Arne Duncan encouraged districts to find alternatives to letting go of the new teachers.

CONTRACT INTEGRITY

Many a new administrator has become embroiled unnecessarily in union issues by overlooking the integrity of the contract. While it is important to insert human elements into contract administration, school leaders should avoid the temptation to disregard the contract in favor of doing someone a favor. Past practices can quickly become nightmares. Many new administrators feel that through charisma and a desire to make caring personal judgments they can disregard the contract and do what they feel is right. Almost without exception, it becomes a hard lesson.

This is coupled with the fact that licensed employees generally seek the independence and freedom of being a professional while working under a union contract. There is often pressure on the administrator to "lighten up and be flexible" rather than taking a hard line on the contract and yet the administrator is bound by the union to maintain the integrity of the agreement.

> One superintendent said "I was certain that we could run our contract management pretty casually because of our relationships. We were small and didn't need the same kind of formal processes that big districts use. We could just talk it out and disregard what the contract said."
>
> "Boy, was I ever wrong on that one. Yes, we are small and pretty laid back, but there were several members of the association who taught me some very hard lessons about the nature or quality of our relationship and its value compared with their own personal well-being in terms of the contract and working conditions. We had to look at some hard decisions about cutting back on staffing levels and also at pay increases and benefits. Before I knew it, the community was involved and they were putting pressure on the board. I was pretty much the Lone Ranger before it was all over."

Some administrators are convinced there are two faculties—the regular teaching staff they see on a daily basis and the union staff whose compensation and working conditions are guided by a negotiated agreement. In the end, they are the same people, and while most of their energies will be focused on their teaching duties, there is the other side which demands careful cultivation and respect.

It is possible to blur the lines and even reduce the potential negative issues surrounding the union agreement, but it is never possible to totally meld the two sides.

Union contracts exist in part to assure fairness and consistency. They also exist to provide an avenue of communication on group issues. An alternative, of course, is to eliminate the group contract and negotiate individually with each staff member. One would want to be very thoughtful before creating such a nightmare and having to negotiate with each staff member.

Imagine how much time would be spent in the staff lounge comparing notes. It would be a far more effective use of time to meet regularly with building representatives or union leaders on a regular basis to discuss ongoing issues and relationships.

The more problems that are resolved before they reach the bargaining table the better. Otherwise the resolution might unnecessarily find its way into contract language. Many new administrators come straight into the position from the same union and somehow believe that they can possibly "retain membership" although not officially. It can't and won't happen.

Making the move doesn't mean one can't continue to be friends, but it does mean that they are no longer just a colleague, but rather their boss and with that comes certain obligations and responsibilities that will provide a measure of separation.

Staff members are generally quicker to acknowledge the new relationship and change of status than are the individuals who move into the leadership position. In fact, many teachers who simply begin training for the principalship experience changes in their relationship with their colleagues.

> *In December of 2003, the Ione Board presented a proposed new working agreement to its licensed staff association. The board prepared a contract which they felt reflected how they felt about the staff and which included a number of unique provisions designed to address the fact Ione has sought to be a different place to work.*
>
> *They prepared and served a prime rib dinner and then unveiled the contract for the staff to study at their leisure. The board also used this opportunity to thank the staff for their faith in the creation of the new school district and for taking a risk in giving up their previous contracts with Morrow County and agreeing to work in Ione even though there was a six-week period during which they were without a contract.*
>
> *One staff member wrote a letter to each individual member of the board, thanking them for the dinner and the recognition, citing that it was a first in a career than spanned more than twenty years.*
>
> *While the dinner was well-received, it didn't preclude many further discussions about contract issues before a new contract was developed.*

In the end, the key to effective relationships with the union is to act in good faith and honor the contract. If a new administrator operates with the idea that he/she has no desire whatsoever to violate the master contract, there is a strong likelihood a positive relationship will develop. While there might be misunderstandings along the way, the intent to do right is a critical factor and key to the creation of an environment of trust and confidence.

FUNDAMENTALS OF PERSONNEL WORK

As with the discussion of curriculum and instruction, this is not an in-depth analysis of human resource management. This section, like most of the others, is primarily a quick overview based upon the past experiences of other administrators. With that in mind, there are some other general topics in the personnel arena that should be pointed out as immediate areas for attention:

Recruitment And Selection of Staff

No decision will have as much influence on the quality of instruction in the school or have such a profound impact on the students as the employment of the best possible staff members. Anyone who has ever had to go through the time-consuming rigor of releasing a mediocre staff member will be more than willing to invest even more time in the process of finding high quality teachers and checking endless references. Every minute invested in resource checking could save hours of grief down the road.

An individual interview process doesn't always have to end in a hire unless the parties agree that the desired qualifications have been met. Because there were ten candidates doesn't always mean that someone needs to be hired. Even if the local university has provided 20 candidates from its graduating class of 200, there is no way of knowing if they are the top 20 or the bottom 20. On rare occasions, it is wiser to piecemeal an alternative solution than to engage the services of someone who could become a long-term problem.

Some small, rural districts have difficulties in attracting teachers who will not eventually be lured away by opportunities in larger districts with more lucrative salary schedules. There are districts that have faced that situation head-on and have accepted the fact that they need good teachers but may not be able to hold-on to them.

In some cases, districts have made a concerted effort to hire the best young, new teachers they can find knowing full well that they may only have their services for a few years. Any given third grade class will only be there for a year and to them, it doesn't make much difference if their teacher is only in town for a year or two—what they care most about is having the best possible teacher during their third grade year. Surprisingly, some of those young stars will end up remaining in the community for a variety of reasons.

As one district put it in its advertisement for a new leader, "Employ and retain the best available certificated and classified staff members and assist them in becoming even more competent through staff development and effective supervision."

Orientation

Many young teachers, particularly those beginning their careers several decades ago, found that when they reported to their first job, they were handed a set of keys and told where the classroom was located—little more.

Today, many school districts are becoming more sophisticated in their orientation processes but unfortunately, they are more apt to conduct the process if there are multiple numbers of new staff. Somehow, when there is just one, the process often gets overlooked and yet, for that individual, the need for orientation is still just as great.

Every principal should set aside at least half-a-day at the outset for orienting new employees and for addressing staff expectations. In addition, periodic follow-ups should also be held prior to important events such as the open house, parent conferences, testing, and filling out the first round of report cards.

Evaluation

Nothing contributes more to the improvement of staff performance than evaluation. As one superintendent/principal noted, *"I once heard the term inspect what you expect if you really care about improved student achievement and improved instructional performance."* This is an important commentary on the value of regular classroom visits as well as the importance of a quality evaluation system. It isn't so much what forms and procedures are used as much as it is the development of a systematic, fair, and consistent procedure mark by trust and open, honest dialogue.

Retention of Staff

Some of those decisions to remain are the product of wise principals who know that it's not enough just to find good teachers, you have to keep them by creating a unique professional environment which makes leaving difficult. Most studies of job satisfaction have shown that compensation is well down the list. Appreciation for a job well done, being part of the decision-making structure, having interesting work, and being respected are all higher up the list.

When a bright new teacher happens to find and marry a local, that just adds to the equation—well, at least now that the rules have changed. In the old days, if a single lady working in a one-room school became married, she had to give-up her teaching position—a strange practice in isolated communities that were strapped for teachers.

A new phenomenon is now at work which positively impacts small, rural districts. That is the issue of quality of life as measured by personal safety. More and more teachers are looking at rural communities as a more desirable place to live and raise a family despite having to sacrifice some of the other conveniences such as nearby box stores and large supermarkets.

Recognition

Staff members like to be recognized for their accomplishments. It need not be a major event. Even a note of acknowledgment for having done something well might be treasured throughout a career. There are legendary stories of classroom teachers who have kept a small note or card taped up in their room for twenty years or more.

At a time when more and more demands are being placed on teachers, principals need to become almost like cheerleaders in the encouragement of good staff performance. The simple act of visiting classrooms regularly to see what the teachers are doing and making positive comments as a part of the visit can produce dividends in terms of improved performance. Some principals make it a habit to begin each morning to make the rounds to greet teachers and students and help get the day off and running in a positive manner. Some elementary principals even go out and meet the buses.

As the demands upon staff become greater, administrators need to be conscious of the impact of new mandates. As one district put it, "leaders need to recognize the increased burden that educational reform places on employees and the efforts made by dedicated certificated and classified staff." Another district suggested that they wished to have a leader who "encourages the District and community to celebrate victories and to express genuine appreciation for those contributing to success."

STAFFING VARIATIONS

As resources in small, rural schools become a greater issue, districts are increasingly looking at staffing alternatives. One district that had traditionally employed a counselor finally came to the conclusion that spending $80,000 (salary and benefits) for a counselor in their small school was simply an expenditure they could no longer afford. They had two needs there were particularly apparent—finding a way to change the behavior of a small group of students who were a continual issue and helping high school students complete college applications.

The district decided to contract with a behavior specialist who was working in a countywide social services position on a part-time basis who would come to the school one day per week and develop a caseload. This had a dramatic impact on the "problem students."

They used recent graduates now in college and community volunteers to deal with the issue of filling out college applications. This "post high school team" expanded its role to work with students as early as the eighth grade in terms of making decisions about high school coursework in order to enhance college preparation. The cost of the contract with the behavior specialist was approximately $9,000.

Another district found it could neither afford nor actually find a part-time music teacher to help at the elementary level. So, they hired the wife of a local minister (who also served as choir director at the church and was an accomplished pianist) to work as a music aide at the school under the supervision of the elementary teachers. The teachers were always nearby during the music period but could address other issues simultaneously.

CONTRACTING FOR SERVICES

A growing number of districts are contracting with their ESD or a cooperative for human resource services. As laws and regulations continue to become more complex, it becomes difficult for personnel working in small schools to remain expert in every area.

By contracting with someone else for such services, they can tap into a larger reservoir of information and secure the services of well-trained individuals whose entire jobs are devoted to the field of human resources. Typically these contracts are minimal in cost and yet the returns are often tremendous—particularly in terms of helping the district protect itself against unintentional oversight or misunderstandings.

One such cooperative venture includes districts of varying sizes. The larger districts, which still have personnel operations of their own, still look to the human resources cooperative to help with recruitment at career fairs, with specialized presentations on training topics for staff, and other generalized presentations.

The smaller districts have need for a broader array of services including job postings, screening of applicants, strategies for organizing and maintaining files, and a host of other specialized human resource functions.

ALTERNATIVE AVENUES IN COMPENSATION

New, young teachers, and even beginning principals, are faced with high costs in terms of licensure requirements. Going from the education required for entry into the profession to continuing licensure certification can be a costly process.

Some boards are becoming flexible in their approach to compensation, recognizing these high costs and helping to contribute in ways that help reduce the financial burden for young staff members. One of the easiest and most obvious ways is to provide educational stipends as a part of the basic agreement with the staff. One rural district, anxious to attract exceptional young teachers, is offering a fully-paid masters degree program as part of the negotiated agreement.

Several other boards are offering education stipends in lieu of salary. Typically, school employees actually see about seventy percent of their basic compensation. When they receive education stipends in lieu of compensation as a part of their contractual agreement, they actually receive 100 percent.

Chapter Fourteen

Instructional Leadership and Student Achievement

Local districts involved in the selection of new educational leaders often leave no question that they are seeking a certain level of knowledge, skills, and experience in the area of improving student achievement.

With the advent of the No Child Left Behind mandates and what some term the "testing frenzy," coupled with several preceding decades of other state and federal mandates, most administrators find themselves in a high stakes race to improve test scores or face the consequences.

Boards of education and hiring committees are equally aware of the challenges facing both superintendents and building principals with regard to instructional leadership and the improvement of student achievement. With that in mind, most searches for new leadership involve expectations surrounding the area of school reform. Some descriptions of the kind of leaders they are seeking include:

- "An understanding and appreciation of effective teaching and learning strategies at all grade levels including the appropriate role of technology in the improvement of learning"
- "Experience in helping foster student achievement by working effectively with staff"
- "Has a successful track record as an educational leader in curriculum alignment, program evaluation, fostering the improvement of student achievement, and applying technology in the instructional program"
- "A school improvement expert – He/she should be familiar with and support effective school reform practices and have the experience to facilitate the district's student achievement and instructional improvement efforts"

- "An extensive knowledge base in educational reform, curriculum, instruction, and assessment"
- "A passion for innovative and creative ideas for improving the educational process, along with a willingness to work with others to ensure their successful adoption and implementation."

Several research studies have shown that where there is an effective school, there exists an effective principal as its leader. This same research shows that schools with the highest student achievement have, among other things, instructionally-assertive principals who are goal-oriented, well-organized, good delegators, and have high expectations for students and staff. As a matter of fact, some research has also shown that without strong leadership, efforts toward improved student achievement are literally doomed to failure.

Other research on the improvement of student achievement speaks directly to the need for sponsoring focused professional development that relates to the instructional mission of the district. The same logic is applied to the purchase of instructional materials.

Principals working in rural areas frequently wear many hats and rarely find themselves supported by a comprehensive curriculum and instruction department. But despite the lack of a support system they still face the same state and federal mandates and standards as their peers in metropolitan districts. In response to this need, there is a movement to bring high quality training and information opportunities to rural areas. Those principals who avail themselves of these opportunities are better able to find success with the sophisticated and complex issues surrounding the reform movements.

Although the Effective Schools Research conducted in the 1980s is considered somewhat passé in this day and age, there are those would argue that it holds just as much merit as it did when it was originally proposed. And it is interesting to note that a multitude of subsequent research studies, as reported in a 2002 study by the University of California at Santa Cruz have confirmed much of those original findings. In terms of student achievement, there are several significant issues that need to be noted in terms of the principal's impact on student achievement—in other words, student achievement in small schools is highest when:

- *the principal is instructionally assertive*
- *the principal is goal-oriented*
- *the principal is well-organized*
- *the principal is a good delegator*
- *the principal holds high expectations for students and staff*

The subsequent studies have also confirmed repeatedly that where there are effective schools, there are effective principals.

The subject of visibility has come up multiple times in discussions of effective leadership in small schools. Nowhere is it more important than as part of the instructional leadership equation. But research on how principals can best spend their time in terms of improved student achievement also reveals that simply being visible is not enough. Something needs to happen as a part of that visibility.

Good principals visit classrooms regularly, review student performance data with classroom teachers, and regularly discuss interventions that are being employed to help improve student achievement. They also seek to create a school-wide environment in which teachers are comfortable coaching and mentoring one another.

> *One of the principals, talking about the subject of classroom visits, could not say enough about the importance of those classroom visits and systematic checks of student progress. This principal reviews test scores with teachers and in making classroom visits, talks, not about overall class activities, but rather the progress of individual pupils in relation to the test data. Said the principal, "this state and the nation in general are possessed with the concept of assessment and testing. We measure almost everything. And yet it is amazing how little attention is paid to what happens with that test data once we have it in hand. There is an unbelievable disconnect between the concept of testing our kids and then actually using what we learn to make instructional decisions."*

Superintendents are equally well-advised to make regular classroom visitations. It is difficult to convince teachers of the importance of raising student achievement without visiting classrooms to inspect what is actually taking place. Once again the admonition, "we can expect what we are willing to inspect" becomes a relevant consideration.

In addition to coping with the growing demands of instructional leadership, many schools in rural areas are also facing a struggle in being able to offer sufficient coursework to meet the needs of their students.

There are growing sources of instructional support that can be incorporated into the array of offerings which are provided to students in small schools. Through technology and improved transportation, accessibility has increased dramatically. Some of the various approaches include:

- Laboratory approaches (Grouping several small classes in the same general subject area into a laboratory setting with the teacher monitoring the work of the students—not unlike the approach found in one-room schools)
- On-line learning—This growing area includes packages offered by private vendors, national networks, statewide offerings, regionally-sponsored classes, and in some cases, classes shared by several high schools in the same district or county.

- Independent study—Tremendous packages are now available for self-guided instruction.
- Use of community members and resources—Some schools have turned to local citizens with particular areas of expertise to help with the instructional process.
- Community colleges—Most areas are attached to a community college and its broad array of offerings. Through dual-credit programs or even straight enrollment, students can secure coursework that may not be regularly available.
- Four-year colleges—Students who happen to live near a four-year college or university can sometimes take advanced coursework by enrolling classes at the college level. This approach is limited, but none-the-less provides yet another option.
- Work experience—Work-study experiences can be used in a variety of ways to expand the curriculum and the training of students. Not only can they be applied to training, they can also be used to provide students with exploratory opportunities in different fields of potential interest without a long-term commitment.
- Inter-district cooperatives—more and more smaller schools are pooling their course offerings and trading enrollment with other nearby schools. Students do not transfer to the other school on a full-time basis but rather participate in specialized courses that their own school does not offer.

One example is a small central Oregon school that offers Vocational Agriculture and FFA for its own students as well as students from three nearby small schools. In several other Oregon instances, one in Umatilla County and another in Union County, high school administrators and boards have identified a group of classes at each school which are open for pooling. Class schedules are built and coordinated at each school to permit joint enrollment.

As enrollment at the South Wasco County High School in Maupin, Oregon has diminished, staff and administrators have continually been in search of ways to continue offering a broader curriculum in the midst of staff declines. One answer to their efforts has been the creation of the "Learning Center," a popular program housed in a modern portable unit adjacent to the old secondary building.

Staffed by a licensed teacher and an aide, the program hosts a steady stream of students with a wide variety of needs. This is where the talented and gifted are introduced to unique courses that their small high school cannot offer.

And this is where students behind in their credits are able to get back on track toward graduation. The Learning Center is also an important part of instruction for the school's growing ELL population. With limited capacity to address the needs of second-language learners, the school has turned to the Learning Center to provide enhanced coursework as part of the transition process.

Students are generally limited to one class per day in the Learning Center, although some have been allowed to take two. The program can handle twenty or more students per period on an almost individualized basis.

South Wasco's Learning Center is not unlike the lab approach being used in other smaller high schools where small enrollments play havoc with scheduling. But it is a concept that could just as well find a home in larger high schools where declining resources have limited the scope of the curriculum.

In the lab approach, a teacher, Business Education for example, may not be able to offer separate classes in bookkeeping, typing, business English, and so forth. Instead, the teacher offers a laboratory approach where small groups of students take various courses during the same period. One group of three or four might be taking beginning bookkeeping while another group is taking advanced coursework in the same subject. Across the room, two students are enrolled in Business English while three more are learning to type. This approach provides an opportunity for students to experience a broader curriculum even if there aren't enough to justify individual classes.

In some larger high schools, this same approach is being used for classes such as foreign languages. In French or even German, for example, where enrollments might be declining, the program can be kept intact through the use of the laboratory approach. A modification is being used in Ione where calculus and pre-calculus are combined since the total enrollment in the two classes is about ten students.

About the Author

George Murdock is a senior associate of Northwest Leadership Associates, a group which has conducted nearly two hundred searches for school leaders in Oregon, Washington, and Idaho. He is also superintendent of the Douglas Education Service District in Roseburg, Oregon, a past president of the Oregon Association of Education Service Districts, and a former executive director of the Oregon Small Schools Association.

In 1997, he was named Washington Superintendent of the Year.

He began his administrative career as vice principal of W. F. West High School in Chehalis, Washington. He became principal in 1974 and in 1982 went to the Walla Walla, Washington School District as deputy superintendent. In 1993, he became superintendent of the Pasco School District, a position he held until 1999 when he became superintendent of the Umatilla-Morrow Education Service District.

During the 2003–2004 school year, he simultaneously served as superintendent of the ESD, the Ione School District, and the Morrow County School District.

He is a graduate of Toledo High School in a class of thirty-seven students, where his father served as superintendent. He has retained a long-term interest in the challenges of small schools.

When he became superintendent of the Umatilla-Morrow ESD in 1999, he began visiting literally every rural school district in Eastern Oregon. At the time, he admitted that he wasn't exactly sure why he had undertaken this adventure, but he felt it was something he needed to do. That undertaking eventually included every rural school district in Oregon and in the fall of 2003, he published a book entitled *Reflecting On A Legacy—170 Years Of Rural Education In Oregon*. It remains the only book on the history of education in Oregon.

He has published several other books, including *"Practical Ideas For Cutting Costs And Ways To Generate Alternative Revenue Sources"* which he co-authored with Tim Adsit. A sequel to that book was published by Rowan and Littlefield in the fall of 2010.

Murdock is a partner in the operation of the Murdock Cattle Company, which is managed on a full-time basis by his son. Their cows, mostly registered Red Angus, run on pastures throughout Umatilla and Morrow Counties in Eastern Oregon.

www.ingramcontent.com/pod-product-compliance
Lightning Source LLC
Chambersburg PA
CBHW031712230426
43668CB00006B/192